ANJERIC

GUEST HOUSE  ST. MARY'S

A view from the Guests' Lounge

- Overlooks Town Beach.
- Minutes' walk to all Hugh Town amenities.
- Close to the Quay, boats to off-islands, churches, museum, shops, and other beaches and bays.
- Licensed dining-room serving varied and ample cuisine.
- All bedrooms have tea and coffee making facilities, and hot and cold drinks are available in the lounge.
- All bedrooms have central heating or electric radiators, most with *en suite* facilities or private bathrooms.
- Friendly, relaxed, smoke-free atmosphere.

OPEN APRIL TO OCTOBER

ANJERIC, The Strand, St. Mary's, Isles of Scilly, TR21 0PS

For further information contact Judy or Barry Archer:
telephone and fax: 01720 422700 or write for illustrated brochure and tariff.

E-mail: judyarcher@yahoo.co.uk

THE ISLES OF SCILLY STANDARD GUIDEBOOK

55th Edition 2004/2005

by

R. L. Bowley

author of *The Fortunate Islands: the Story of the Isles of Scilly* and of *Scilly at War.*

INTRODUCTION

The Isles of Scilly are today the most fortunate of all the islands around Britain's coasts, with clean seas and beaches, wonderful scenery, welcoming inhabitants, excellent accommodation, and a climate which is one of Britain's warmest in winter and sunniest in summer.

The islands form a group of five* inhabited islands and fifty-one uninhabited, smaller islands situated twenty-eight miles west-south-west of Land's End. They are very small – the largest island, St. Mary's, is less than three miles across at its widest part and only ten miles around its coastline. For the winter visitor, Scilly offers early flowers – which are the islands' principal export – and a mild climate, which makes their growth possible; in summer, the visitor can enjoy sea, sun, sand, and relative solitude. For the holidaymaker, the small size of the islands possesses several advantages: there is more coastline to explore than in any mainland seaside resort; the beaches are uncrowded because there are so many from which to choose; and even on a breezy day shelter can usually be found close at hand on a leeward shore.

The sea water is rather cold for bathing, especially early in the year, but very inviting in appearance. In strong sunlight its colour is blue, rather than the dull, greenish hue around most of the coasts of England. The water around Scilly is also clear because it is free from the discolouring effects of muddy rivers and, when the surface is still, it is so transparent that the sea-bed is often visible at depths of several fathoms – ideal for underwater swimming. The translucency of the water is matched by the clarity of the atmosphere, which is relatively free from pollution by smoke and dust. As a result the sunlight is often very bright, and this helps to account for some of the glorious colourings in Scilly. But caution is advisable when sunbathing, for salt, sea breezes may lull some visitors into a false sense of security leading to unprotected exposure and painful burns.

Scilly's beaches are very clean compared with most mainland beaches, and many have fine white sand which glistens in the sunlight. The sand on some beaches is so fine that it was at one time exported from the islands and used to dry ink before blotting paper had been invented. The beaches vary, too; some shelve steeply and are

**Strictly six, if the Gugh, on which there are two houses, is regarded as separate from St. Agnes. The names of the fifty-six islands are listed on page 75.*

Mount Royal Hotel

Chyandour Cliff, Penzance, Cornwall, TR18 3LQ

AA **Telephone/Fax: 01736 362233** **RAC**

E-mail: mountroyal@btconnect.com Website: www.s-h-systems.co.uk/hotels/mouroyal.html

Mount Royal Hotel is a Georgian, part Victorian house and has been a family run hotel for over thirty years. The hotel faces the sea and overlooks the entrance of Penzance harbour with panoramic views of St. Michael's Mount and the Lizard peninsula.

Spacious bedrooms with en suite facilities, premier rooms with spectacular sea views. Elegant and original Victorian dining room, separate tables, silver service.

Private parking in our own grounds with lock-up garages available for persons visiting the Isles of Scilly. Close to the harbour, and nearest hotel to the heliport, five minutes' walk to town, coach and rail terminus.

ISLES OF SCILLY TRAVELLERS WELCOME

Bed and breakfast terms from £30·00 per person. Weekly terms available. Individual lock up garage in hotel grounds, £5·00 per night or £35·00 per week.

Resident proprietors: Mr. and Mrs. J. Cox.

ARTS AND CRAFTS

Among the many arts and crafts studios and workshops in Scilly which visitors are recommended to see are the Isles of Scilly Pottery on the Garrison, John Bourdeaux's Pottery in Old Town Lane for ceramics, Elm Studio, the Isles of Scilly Perfumery, Susan Woof at Porthloo, the Phoenix Stained Glass Studio at Porthmellon, the Man of War in The Strand for a collection of maritime objects, the art work at the studios next to Glandore Guest House at Porthloo including that of Stephen Morris, the Rosehill Art Studio for paintings and Rosehill Wood Crafts workshop for wooden gifts, Chris Smith's studio at Old Town for watercolours, the Rat Island workshop of Keith Buchanan for canvas products, Peter Smith's studio at Porthloo for oils and pastels, and the Studio Wingletang in Thorofare in Hugh Town. On the off-islands are: on Bryher, the Golden Eagle Studio; on St. Martin's, Little Arthur, North Farm Gallery and Middle Town Gallery, run by Mandy Mills, papermaker and printmaker; and on Tresco is the Tresco Gallery at New Grimsby.

ideal for bathing, while on others it is possible at dead low water to walk nearly half a mile out to sea on dry sand. Many beaches are particularly rewarding for the large number and variety of attractive seashells (including cowries) which can be found when beachcombing along the high-tide mark, and there is an interesting collection of them on view in the museum in Hugh Town. From all the beaches in Scilly bathing is safe, with two exceptions – and then only at high tide. The two places where caution should be exercised are both sand bars, one connecting the Gugh with St. Agnes, the other at Pelistry, joining Toll's Island to St. Mary's. When the sea covers these bars, bathing may become unsafe because of currents.

Another attraction of Scilly is the comparative absence of noise except for the natural sounds of the sea and the birds. This is especially apparent on the off-islands where there are tractors but few cars. It produces a calmer atmosphere with a slower pace of life which, it is said, helps the careworn visitor to unwind from the stresses and strains of his mainland existence. As one visitor put it: 'There is a magic on the islands; once you have been to Scilly you feel you belong there and keep going back to seek its peace.'

For so small an area it is surprising how much good walking can be obtained. There is a great deal of open heathland, ideal for those who like soft, springy turf, glorious and changing views, and some stimulating scrambling. But the islands have no high cliffs, and the highest point, Telegraph, rises only to 165 feet above mean sea level. There is scope for rock climbing, however, particularly at Peninnis, St. Mary's, and at Shipman Head, north of Bryher. The granite rock is lighter in colour and more sparkling than much of that on the mainland, and, when dry, is sure underfoot.

To many visitors the primary delights of Scilly are the boat trips: not just once around the bay, which is all most mainland seaside resorts can offer, but adventurous expeditions to unfrequented islets to see seals, sharks, and less common seabirds in their natural surroundings; or to uninhabited islands to land for the day where no other footprints mar the sandy bays; or to explore caves such as Underland Girt on remote White Island off St. Martin's, or Piper's Hole on Tresco; or, in calm weather, to visit a distant lighthouse, such as the Bishop Rock, looking at seals among the Western Rocks on the way. It is this form of interest which gives to boating in Scilly a character all of its own. Regular summer services are run from St. Mary's Quay, and in suitable weather offer a wide choice of trips. Each of the larger islands deserves a day's visit at least, for each has its particular mood and charm. St. Agnes is wild and rugged on its western shores, a fitting bulwark to the elements, yet the Cove has one of the most popular bathing beaches. St. Martin's is soft and sweet-scented with panoramic views of sea, sand, and heather, which in strong sunlight produce striking contrasts of vivid colour. Tresco, with its caves, fine beaches, and sub-tropical garden, is a common favourite; while Bryher has both the ruggedness of Shipman Head and the placidity of Rushy Bay. St. Mary's, which is larger than Tresco, Bryher, and St. Martin's put together, also has much to offer: Bar Point, Pelistry, Porth Hellick, Peninnis, and the Garrison are all attractive and relatively unfrequented. By Scillonian standards, these areas are regarded as crowded when their human populations reach double figures.

COMMUNICATIONS

(1) By Sea

The Isles of Scilly Steamship Co. Ltd., which is largely owned by the islanders, possesses one passenger ferry, *Scillonian III*, a vessel of just over a thousand tons built in 1977, and one freighter, the blue-hulled, *Gry Maritha,* which makes a thrice weekly crossing to Scilly from Penzance. The first *Scillonian* served Scilly from 1926 to 1955, the second from 1955 to 1977 and *Scillonian III* since then; she was given a £1·7m refurbishment at Plymouth in 1999.

Scillonian III sails from Penzance to St. Mary's daily (except Sundays) from the end of March to the beginning of November carrying passengers to and from the Islands. The 42-mile journey takes approximately 2 hours and 40 minutes. This day sea-trip is the finest and most interesting to be had from any port in Cornwall, and can be highly recommended to visitors to Cornwall in pleasant weather – it is Penzance's treasure. Coach trips from Newquay and from St. Ives to the *Scillonian III* are also available in the season.

Scillonian III was launched in 1977 by HRH the Prince of Wales, and is licensed to carry a maximum of 600 passengers at a comfortable speed of sixteen knots. The normal departure time from Penzance in the season is at 09.15 (but different on Saturdays) with return at 16.30 from St. Mary's, thus allowing for those making the day trip to Scilly upwards of 4 hours to go ashore and gain a taste of the Islands. Travel times may need confirming by telephoning Scilly Travel (0845 710 5555) or visiting their ticket-office on the weighbridge near the head of Lighthouse Quay – *Scillonian III's* departure point.

There is an impressive exhibition of pictures of Scilly on her main deck, and a cafe-lounge and bar. On the ourward journey, passengers frequently like to admire the views of the Cornish coast on the starboard side, with the attractive village of Mousehole (and the mouth of the cave just to its west which some believe gave the village its name) and, further along the coast, Porthcurno with the Minack Theatre to its west dramatically carved on its granite cliff site.

Scillonian III usually sounds her siren half-an-hour before sailing – both from Penzance and from St. Mary's – and, when approaching St. Mary's, sounds her siren about five minutes before reaching Hugh Town harbour to warn craft of her approach. When casting off from St. Mary's quay for the return journey to Penzance, she usually sounds three short blasts on her siren, which is an international signal warning nearby craft that she is going astern.

(2) By Air

There is a regular air service to the Isles of Scilly operated by BI's two American-built, 32-seat, Sikorsky S61 helicopters flying from the heliport at Eastern Green, which is off the main A30 road under a mile east of Penzance. A coach service runs between Penzance railway station and the heliport, where there is a secured open car park for which there is a fee. Refreshments are available at the café in the heliport lounge. There are no flights on Sundays, but on weekdays there are flights from Penzance to St. Mary's and to Tresco.

The helicopter is amphibious for safety and is capable of lifting two tons. Landing and take-off are very smooth and feel safe because both are made at zero forward speed. The helicopter has two engines and can continue to fly even if one stops. Each rotor-blade is thirty-one feet long. Passengers enjoy panoramic views from the cabin. The helicopter cruises at about 120 knots, with the flight from Penzance taking about twenty minutes.

Seat reservations are advisable and can be made through any travel agency or by contacting Seat Reservations, British International, The Heliport, Penzance

(telephone: 01736 363871), or British International, The Airport, St. Mary's, Isles of Scilly (telephone: 01720 422646). On St. Mary's a coach runs between the airport and Hugh Town and connects with every flight. There are a number of flights every weekday throughout the year. Thirty-three pounds of baggage is permitted for each seat passenger, and excess luggage will be carried at the advertised rates, if there is room, or it can be sent by sea (see page 11). Excellent air services are also run to the Isles of Scilly by Isles of Scilly Skybus Ltd., which fly aircraft from Land's End Aerodrome at St. Just, the flight taking only about fifteen minutes or less, and there is secured parking for cars at the aerodrome for which there is a fee.

Skybus also operate flights from Bristol once daily from Monday to Friday, and twice daily on Saturdays (there is no Sunday service). Exeter operates the same number of flights as Bristol, and both these airports have good motorway and trunk-road access. A service from Southampton operates 4 flights weekly throughout the holiday season. A quick and convenient direct train link to Southampton Parkway (which is at the airport) from Waterloo means that visitors can be in Scilly just 4 hours after leaving London or the South East of England.

Flights from Land's End and Newquay operate daily (except Sundays) all the year round at regular intervals. Flights from Land's End are serviced by the 8-seater Britten-Norman Islanders with 19-seater DHC-6 Twin Otters flying from other airports.

Details of flight times and prices can be obtained from the Isles of Scilly Travel, Quay Street, Penzance, TR18 4BZ, Tel: 0845 710 5555, or www.ios-travel.co.uk

(3) By Air from London

It is possible to fly from London Gatwick to Newquay with Air South West. There are 4 flights daily, details of which can be obtained from their reservations department on 0870 241 8202 or on their website: www.airsouthwest.com

Ryanair also operates a twice-daily service from London Stansted to Newquay, telephone 0871 246 0000 or visit www.ryanair.com for more details.

It is advisable to check the flight times and availability with the operators in case of changes.

(4) By Launch to the Off-Islands

The Isles of Scilly Steamship Co. operates the cargo/passenger launch *Lyonesse Lady* on behalf of the Council of the Isles of Scilly, connecting the other inhabited islands with St. Mary's. In addition, passenger launches are operated by St. Mary's Boatmen's Association. These boats leave St. Mary's Quay from 10.00 and 14.00 in the summer, and tickets can be obtained at the ticket kiosk on the Old Quay, St. Mary's. Notices advertising the trips are displayed in Hugh Street and on the Old Quay, and are revised daily at about 08.45. Launches are also operated by independent boatmen (see P. 19).

(5) On St. Mary's

There are a number of taxis on St. Mary's (see page 75 for phone numbers) and two Island carriers deliver luggage, Richard Hand (01720 423007) and Island Carriers (01720 422662). In most holiday seasons there is a scheduled bus service on St. Mary's connecting the country areas with Hugh Town, the bus making a round trip of the island via Telegraph.

book on line now
www.islesofscillyhelicopter.com
Fly by
British International
helicopter
to the beautiful Isles of Scilly
Direct flights to St Mary's & Tresco
Celebrating
40
years
Flying to St Mary's
2004 - British International
Flying to Tresco
Celebrating
21
years
Call Reservations on 01736 363871
British International

ACCOMMODATION

Hugh Town, St. Mary's, is the capital of the Isles of Scilly and the focus of communications in the islands. It contains six **hotels** and several **guest-houses**, but the accommodation is insufficient to cater for the number of visitors who wish to stay in the summer months, and it is therefore inadvisable to arrive without booking accommodation beforehand. An enquiry to the Tourist Information Centre, St. Mary's, Isles of Scilly, TR21 0JL (tel: 01720 422536), will bring a brochure with a list of hotels and of other available accommodation, and Bryher Boat Services, Jenford, Bryher, Isles of Scilly, TR23 0PR, tel: 01720 422892, produce an excellent inclusive holiday brochure. **Caravans** and **dormobiles** are not permitted on the islands and, as there are only eleven miles of narrow roads on St. Mary's, active visitors are advised not to bring **cars**. These may be left in Penzance in the open at the Harbour Car Park, or at the Penzance Heliport by visitors travelling by helicopter, or parked at Land's End Aerodrome by those travelling by Skybus. There is security fencing at the last two, and all three make charges.

THE DUCHY OF CORNWALL, LOCAL GOVERNMENT and the WILDLIFE TRUST

By 2000, the Duchy of Cornwall owned about 147,000 acres, some in Cornwall but much in other parts of England, generating in 1998 about £6·4m in rents, etc. (£2·4m for tax, £2·5m for official expenses, £1·5m for the Prince of Wales). The Duchy has owned title to the Isles of Scilly since 1337, except that, after 1949, it sold the freehold of most of its houses in Hugh Town to sitting tenants. In 1570, the Duchy had leased Scilly to Francis Godolphin, whose family continued to hold the lease almost uninterruptedly until relinquishing it in 1831. Local government was administered through a Council of Twelve, usually presided over by the Godolphins' steward, as the Godolphins increasingly became absentee proprietors.

A Select Vestry took over from the Council of Twelve in 1832, originally composed of thirty-four prominent Scillonians meeting once a month. Then, from 1834, Augustus Smith was granted a lease of Scilly from the Duchy, followed by his nephew T. A. Dorrien Smith from 1872 to 1918, and both were content to rule Scilly through the Select Vestry; then, in 1891, as a consequence of the Local Government Act of 1888, the democratically-elected Isles of Scilly Council was established and took over most local government functions, including those of a county council, although initially Dorrien Smith was its permanent chairman. Today, Robert Dorrien Smith leases only Tresco from the Duchy.

Scilly is designated as an Area of Outstanding Natural Beauty, the coast as a Heritage Coast and the waters around as a Marine Park. This helps the work of the Council of the Isles of Scilly and the Duchy of Cornwall who have always taken a longterm view of the well-being of the islands, and endeavoured to prevent them from being spoilt by hasty development. The Duchy is administered locally by a Land Steward from offices at Hugh House, The Garrison, St. Mary's, but in 1985 the Duchy handed over the management of the untenanted land in Scilly to the newly-formed Isles of Scilly Wildlife (formerly Environmental) Trust on a 99 year lease. This Trust is a registered charity under the patronage of the Duke of Cornwall and is dependent

The blow-hole in action on Peninnis. Spray emerging from deep below the rocks can drench an unwary passer-by. *Photo: Keith Dibley*

for income upon grants and voluntary contributions. It was established to take over the protection and enhancement of the natural environment in Scilly. The Trust has sixteen trustees – who all reside locally – and two paid staff, who can be contacted at the Trust's Office in Hugh Town at Carn Thomas.

DOGS ON ST. MARY'S

Dogs are banned from Porthcressa, Porthmellon and Old Town beaches from May to September and their fouling of footways is an offence. The Council appointed a dog warden in 1989 and poop scoops (whoopsie kits) are available free from the Tourist Information Centre in Hugh Street on St. Mary's, nearly opposite the paper shop.

CHURCHES AND CHAPELS

There are Church of England churches on the five main islands, Methodist on St. Mary's and St. Martin's, and Roman Catholic on St. Mary's. Regular services are held in the church of St. Mary the Virgin (see notice board outside the church). At the Methodist Church, services on Sundays from April to September (inclusive) are at 11.00 and 20.00. A short Epilogue Service by candlelight is usually held at Old Town Church on Sundays at 20.15, April to September, but see notice-boards.

LOCAL AUTHORITIES

The islands are administered by a council composed of twenty-one councillors, thirteen from St. Mary's, two from Tresco, two from St. Martin's, two from Bryher, and two from St. Agnes. The Council can be described as 'having the size of a parish with powers and responsibilities of a county'. It is responsible for education, agriculture, welfare, the police (there are four policemen during the holiday season and two in winter), and town and country planning. In addition, there is a National Health Executive Council, and the Cornwall and Isles of Scilly Health Authority maintains a small but well-equipped hospital on St. Mary's. Two doctors, a veterinary surgeon, and a dentist are resident on St. Mary's. Other authorities include the Royal National Lifeboat Institution; Trinity House concerned with lighthouses and buoys; the Coastguards with a station at Telegraph; and an Agricultural Executive. There are, however, no arrangements for MOT tests in Scilly, and no speed limits as yet on the roads other than the statutory limit of 60 m.p.h., although, before the 2nd World War, there was a 20 m.p.h. speed limit in Hugh Town.

TELEPHONE, ELECTRICITY, TELEVISION

Scillonia telephone exchange is fully automatic, the inhabited off-islands being linked to St. Mary's by undersea cables. Telephone calls to the mainland are sent by radio and, between Scilly and the Penzance area, are charged only as local calls.

In 1989, after a submarine cable had been laid from Whitesand Bay near Land's End to Porthcressa at a cost of £7m, Scilly was connected to the national grid and Scilly's electricity prices were reduced to mainland tariffs. But the old generating station at the foot of Buzza Hill has been retained in serviceable use in case of a breakdown. Mains electricity cables connecting the inhabited off-islands with St. Mary's were laid in 1985. Good terrestrial television reception is provided in Scilly by a relay station at Telegraph.

WATER, SEWAGE, REFUSE

Scilly's average annual rainfall is about thirty-five inches, and, in the past, there have been threats of water shortages on St. Mary's when, in dry periods in high summer, up to about 140,000 gallons a day can be used. Now, over 180,000 gallons a day can be pumped from boreholes in addition to 55,000 gallons a day from a desalination plant installed at Mount Todden in 1992. Blending the water from both sources has had the incidental beneficial effect of reducing the level of nitrates in the supply to within EEC requirements. Reservoir capacity at Telegraph, Buzza Hill and The Garrison has been increased to 257,000 gallons, and these improvements mean that St. Mary's now has a better water supply.

Sewage from Hugh Town is pumped into the sea at Morning Point, the tidal current in St. Mary's Sound taking most of the outflow away from the islands. Refuse on St. Mary's is disposed of by an incinerator in the Lower Moors. Much of the refuse from the off-islands, other than Tresco, is also incinerated here. An exhaust-gas cleaning facility was added to this Porthmellon Incinerator Plant in 2002 and helps in the disposal of much of Scilly's rubbish. With the help of EU finance, this is making Scilly a good model in energy recovery by recycling waste to produce usable products – such as waste food into good compost – which helps in replacing soil nutrients lost in commercial flower growing.

SUMMER ENTERTAINMENT on the water in Scilly

(a) Launch Trips leave St. Mary's Quay to visit the off-islands at 10.15 each morning (to Tresco from 10.00), and each of the inhabited off-islands has launches making similar trips for holidaymakers staying there.

(b) Special Trips include: (1) A voyage to the ***Bishop Rock*** lighthouse via the Western Rocks to see the seals and seabirds, with the option of landing on St. Agnes on the return journey: (2) A trip around the ***Eastern Islands*** to see the wildlife – no guarantee given that they will be seen, but they usually are – landing on St. Martin's for the remainder of the day: (3) A trip to the ***Norrard Rocks*** landing on Bryher or Tresco afterwards: (4) A trip to ***Round Island***, Teän, St. Helen's, and including Men-a-vaur, where some puffins are likely to be seen from May until late in July.

(c) Evening and other trips include: (1) ***The Shearwater Special***, which aims to find the elusive shearwaters which, in season, commonly assemble towards dusk in rafts on the sea, awaiting their opportunity to return to their burrows on small islands such as Annet without being intercepted by the predatory Great and Lesser Black-backed Gulls: (2) ***A Cruise in the Past***, which is around the islands to see sites of archaeological and historical interest, usually with a commentary given by a local historian: (3) ***Seabird Special***, which is a two-hour trip to visit rocks and small islands to see many varieties of seabirds, usually accompanied by a commentary from a local ornithologist: (4) ***St. Agnes Evening Trip***, which involves an evening stroll on St. Agnes followed by singsong and sustenance at the Turk's Head: (5) ***Samson Trip***, which, in high summer on a pleasant evening, provides a landing on this uninhabited island: (6) ***Gig Racing*** trips on Wednesday and Friday evenings in summer in suitable weather to follow the gigs: (7) ***Fishing Trips***, which are organised in good weather in the summer with equipment provided – see noticeboards on the quay, or visit the Tourist Information Office in the old Wesleyan Chapel in Garrison Lane (see map on centre pages) or telephone them (01720 422536 or fax 01720 422049): (8) ***Round St. Mary's*** is a circumnavigation of St. Mary's.

The boat trips in Scilly are not just more numerous than elsewhere but of wide interest, with the skippers putting themselves out to provide both information and humour; often they manage to convey a sense of adventure, almost as if each trip was their first time of making it.

Independent Launches of St. Mary's

Launch Name	*Skipper/owner and his phone number*	*Tickets, Bookings etc:*
Calypso II *(private hire)*	Tim Fortey tel: 422187 Mobile 07778-198454	Tidelines *(shop opposite paper shop)*
Blue Hunter	Paul Osborne Tel: 423 377	Sports Mode *(shop by the Park)*
Kestrel	Martin Jenkins tel: 422251 or mobile 07767 803973	Sports Mode *(fishing and private hire)*
Crusader	Paul Hicks 422028 or mobile 07748 243122	Bourdeaux Shop Travel 1st Class in a 31-foot modern vessel
Pettifox	Alfred Hicks tel: 422917 *(after 6 pm)* 422511 *(Estate office)*	Tidelines. Sailing vessel (gaff cutter) built in Scilly in 1992. Owned by Tresco Estate

On the off-islands, Bryher Boat Services, which operate the *Firethorn*, *Falcon*, *Cyclone* and *Faldore*, can be contacted on 422886 or 422892 (see p. 65), St. Agnes Boat Services, which run the catamaran *Spirit of St. Agnes* and the *Vanguard* can be contacted on 422704, and St. Martin's Boat Services, which run the *Voyager of St. Martin's* and the *Enterprise*, can be contacted on 422814 or mobile 07831 585365.

(2) Tours (St. Mary's)

See page 75 for coach and car tours.

Island Wildlife Tours take place from March to October, and consist of walks accompanied by a naturalist. Weather permitting, they take place several times a week, and start at 09.45 from near the noticeboard close to the Boatmen's Association kiosk on the Old Quay, St. Mary's. Popular walks are on the off-islands, and details of these are on the naturalists' noticeboard on St. Mary's Quay. The tours' leader is Will. Wagstaff (tel: 422212), who is the local ornithologist. Half-day walks – at a leisurely pace – are also organised and led by archaeologist Katharine Sawyer (please phone 01720 423326).

(3) Lectures, Slideshows, and other regular entertainments in Hugh Town in the summer months (times and days may vary)

MONDAYS:	(1) **Slideshow of the Islands** at 20.15 in the Methodist Church Hall in Hugh Town. (2) **Underwater World** slideshow at 20.30 in the Church Hall next to the Museum.
WEDNESDAYS:	**Slideshow of the Islands** (alternative programme) given at 20.15 in the Methodist Church Hall. Women's gig-racing night. At 20.15 on some Wednesday evenings, selections from video archives are played in the Museum.
THURSDAYS:	**Shipwrecks in Scilly**. One of a series of four slideshows held in the Methodist Church Hall at 20.15, except for the third Thursday of the month when the show is held on the Tuesday of that week.
FRIDAYS:	Men's gig-racing night.
SATURDAYS:	**Wildlife on Scilly**. A slideshow by naturalist Will. Wagstaff, one of two alternate programmes at 20.15 in the Church Hall, which is next to the Museum. (Check notice-boards for changes to these shows)

(4) Museum, Library

The Isles of Scilly **Museum** in Church Street is open in the summer, Monday to Saturday, 10.00 to 12.00, 13.30 to 16.30 and 19.30 to 21.00. The **Library,** in the former Wesleyan Chapel in Garrison Lane, is open Monday 15.00 to 19.00, Wednesday 15.00 to 17.00, Thursday 11.00 to 15.00, Saturday 10.00 to 12.00. Times may vary but are posted on the door.

(5) Music, Plays, Riding, Tennis, Squash

St. Mary's Choral Society **Operatic Productions**, Scillonian Entertainers' **Variety Shows**, and St. Mary's Theatre Club **Plays** take place in the Town Hall at intervals. There is a **tennis court** on the Garrison – enquiries should be made at the Dairy in The Strand. There are **riding lessons** available at Atlantic View, High Lane, St. Mary's, and **squash** at the court at Porthmellon which is open from 09.00 to 22.00, with payment by slot-machine for twenty-minute sessions.

(6) Annuals

Church fêtes take place on the first Wednesday in August in the Chaplaincy garden and, later, on other islands. There is also the **Crowning of the May Queen** in The Park, Hugh Town, and **Lifeboat Week** is in late July. The **St. Helen's Pilgrimage** usually takes place on the nearest convenient Sunday to the 8th August. A company of visiting actors performs a Shakespeare play in the Chaplaincy garden on St. Mary's, and also on Tresco, each year in August.

GIGS IN SCILLY

Gig racing is the most popular sport in Scilly and a great attraction to visitors. Throughout the summer on Wednesday evenings (women), and on Friday evenings (men), compete in races in the six-oared gigs when the weather is suitable. The start is usually from Nut Rock off Samson, with the finish at St. Mary's Quay, the racing gigs being closely followed all the way by launches packed with spectators urging on their favourite crews. The gigs are maintained almost entirely from the proceeds of raffles and collections.

Some of the gigs are well over a hundred years old, and were originally built to carry Scillonian pilots to approaching ships. They were also used to rescue people from wrecks, for salvage work and for lighthouse relief. In the 19th century each of the inhabited islands possessed several gigs, and the racing then was in earnest to be the first to put a pilot on a vessel wanting assistance up the English or Bristol Channels, or on one seeking shelter within the islands or awaiting a favourable wind.

The oldest gig still racing in Scilly is the *Bonnet*, built about 1830 by the original gig-builders, the Peters family of St. Mawes. The *Bonnet* is reputedly so named after the practice of a St. Martin's woman who used to wave her headgear at the crew to bring them luck when they set off seeking pilotage. The *Bonnet* races now with a St. Mary's crew, as does the *Golden Eagle* (1870). Four recently-built replicas of old craft are *Serica* (St. Mary's), *Dolphin* (St. Martin's), *Men-a-vaur* (Tresco), *Nornour* (St. Mary's). The *Czar*, now rowed by a crew from Tresco and Bryher, was originally known as 'the cut-throat gig' because she was given a seventh oar as a means of outpacing the *Golden Eagle*. Other gigs that have raced recently in Scilly include the *Shah* (St. Agnes) and the *Slippen* (St. Mary's) and the *Islander*, built in Scilly in 1989 of Cornish elm. For several years now, in May, Scilly has played host to the World Gig-Racing Championships, and each year the event attracts more entries. In May, 2001, over 70 gigs competed, with Caradon's gig, *Mary Newman*, winning for the seventh time, and Scilly's gig, *Tregarthen,* coming second.

In the 2003 World Gig Championships in Scilly, the Men's Final was once again won by the swift mainland gig *Mary Newman* (5th in the Ladies Final) with the new gig *Penlee Point* second and the Scillonian gig *Tregarthens* third (1st in the Ladies Final). The *Islander* was 14th and *Golden Eagle* 16th out of 74 gigs which actually competed. A heavy sea was running and some gigs experienced difficulty reaching the start position off St. Agnes, one even breaking a paddle and retiring before the start.

One of the old pilot-gigs, the *Klondyke*, built in 1873, has now been restored and fully rigged, and forms the centre-piece in the Isles of Scilly Museum.

Hugh Town is built on a low, sandy isthmus joining the two parts of St. Mary's, and loo somewhat vulnerable to the slowly rising sea level currently estimated at about 1·8 mm a ye but the American continent is estimated to be moving away from Scilly (and from the rest Britain) by nearly ten times that amount annually. *Photo: Sue Dibl*

Gig racing on a summer evening (weather permitting) is the most popular sport in Sci nowadays. *Photo: Keith Dibl*

RESTAURANTS AND CAFÉS

On St. Mary's there are many restaurants and cafés. These include the Pilot's Gig, Porthcressa Inn and Restaurant, Scillonian Club, The Galley, The Mermaid, The Bishop and Wolf, Hotel Godolphin, Atlantic Hotel, Star Castle Hotel, Tregarthen's Hotel, Bell Rock Hotel, Juliet's Garden (just up a path from Porthloo Lane), the Airport Buffet, Old Town Café, Tolman Café, Longstone Heritage Centre Café, the Atlantic Inn, Kavorna Café, Scilly Plaice (formerly the Corner House), the dibble and grub, Chez Michel (Nornour) and the Golf Club. In addition, each of the inhabited off-islands has restaurants and cafés. On St. Mary's there are five public houses – The Mermaid, The Bishop and Wolf, The Porthcressa Inn and Restaurant, Atlantic Inn and The Old Town Inn – and there are bars at Star Castle Hotel, Tregarthen's Hotel, St. Mary's Hall Hotel and Hotel Beachcomber. At the Scillonian Club there are two licensed bars; on the off-islands there are the Seven Stones, Little Arthur Café, Polreath Tea Rooms and St. Martin's Hotel on St. Martin's, Covean Café, Coastguard Café and the Turk's Head on St. Agnes, Hell Bay Hotel and Fraggle Rock Restaurant on Bryher, and, on Tresco, Quay Shop Café, the Gardens Café, the New Inn and the Island Hotel. There are also off-licences at the Post Office Stores on St. Agnes, St. Martin's and Bryher.

ST. MARY'S

St. Mary's is the main island in Scilly, and is of pleasing, if unusual, proportions, consisting of two unequal but relatively high parts, each roughly round in shape. These are joined by a low, narrow isthmus on which stands the principal settlement of Hugh Town, separating two sandy beaches facing in opposite directions, both within easy reach of the principal hotels and guest-houses. The beach on the south side is Porthcressa, a magnificent, sheltered bay, where bathing is pleasant and safe at all tides, and where visiting yachts sometimes anchor in the bay in the summer months. On the north side is Town Beach, cluttered with ropes and boats towards its western end, but becoming a pleasant strand of sand east of the Rechabite slip, and providing an absorbing view of the busy harbour as a bonus interest. Beyond the lifeboat slip are Porthmellon, Porth Thomas (Shark's Pit) and Porthloo, all fine beaches within a few minutes' walk of one another. On the south side are sheltered bays at Old Town and Porth Hellick; to complete the choice of beaches, there are – on the other side of the island – Pelistry, Watermill Cove and Bar Point.

Hugh Town has over two dozen shops, including a chemist, a newsagent, two butchers, two photographic shops, clothes shops, two hairdressers, a launderette at Porthcressa, a baker, a hardware store and ships' chandlers. Co-operative Retail Services Ltd. (Cornwall) has a shop in Hugh Street, and there are two banks – Lloyds and Barclays. Newspapers are sent to Scilly by air from Penzance and are on sale on the day of publication, except on Sundays when there are usually no flights, so Sunday newspapers may not be available until Monday morning. Scilly's own magazine is *The Scillonian* – published biannually and available from the newsagent, C. Mumford, Hugh Street, St. Mary's. It enables visitors and islanders to keep in touch with Scilly's affairs. Early closing is on Wednesday, and lunch-time is early in Scilly, with some shops closing at midday and re-opening at 13.30.

There is a sporting nine-hole golf course on St. Mary's, with a modern clubhouse and bar which are open to non-members 10.00 to 17.00, Monday to Friday.

St. Mary's also has a Choral Society, a Rotary Club, a Squash Club, a Rugby Club and a Football Club with two rival teams – the Woolpack Wanderers and the Garrison Gunners. Pool, snooker, tombola (bingo), bridge and whist are played at the Scillonian Club, where visitors are most welcome. The Scillonian Sailing Club is an RYA Recognised Teaching Establishment. Local members sail for recreation or instruction three evenings a week, and race Toppers one evening. Visitors are welcome as temporary members. Details and contact telephone number will be found on the club notice-board, next to the Island Carriers at Porthmellon.

In the Middle Ages, Old Town, protected by Castle Ennor, was the principal centre of population on St. Mary's. The castle was mentioned in the Patent Rolls as early as 1306, when, whoever held the Islands from the King, had to pay the upkeep of 12 men-at-arms at the castle; but when Star Castle was constructed in 1593 as a defence measure against possible Spanish attack, most of the population in due course shifted to Hugh Town. The original quay was built in 1603, extended to Rat Island in 1835, and considerably extended in 1889, with a further small extension during repairs to the quay in 1994. St. Mary's Road is fairly deep, but the harbour is tidal and no large vessel can use it at low water. *Scillonian III*, which draws nine and a half feet, can reach the quay at all except low spring tides. The Old Quay is a fine example of drystone walling.

Now, Old Town with over 300 residents is developing again into a village in its own right, with two cafés, a shop, and public house.

WALKS ON ST. MARY'S

The Garrison Walk

The short, circular walk around the Garrison is traditionally an evening stroll on account of the fine sunsets to be observed over Samson in suitable weather. Passing through the Garrison Gate, which was built in 1742 as part of the garrison wall which extends around the promontory, the road leads past the old powder-house on the left up the hill to Star Castle, an Elizabethan fort which was built in the form of an eight-pointed star. Its formidable ramparts are eighteen feet thick, and a dry moat runs around the outside of them. The house in the centre is also star-shaped and contains some fine, granite fireplaces. Star Castle was converted into an hotel in May 1933, when the first visitor to lunch was the Prince of Wales, before he became King Edward VIII and, later, Duke of Windsor. The castle dungeons have been made into a bar. Outside the entrance of Star Castle is the seat given by Richard Branson in 1986 in appreci-ation of the courtesy and assistance he received from islanders after his successful attempt on the Atlantic Crossing record by his power-boat *Virgin Atlantic Challenger II* – the Bishop Rock being the finishing post of this race across the Atlantic.

Continuing past the castle, straight on leads to the sports field, but bearing right leads down to old gun batteries constructed at the turn of the century, and to **Woolpack Point** where there are four old cannon. Other old cannon (some from HMS *Colossus* wrecked off Samson in 1798) are on the Quay, St. Mary's, where their barrels, pointing skywards, have been embedded in the pier to serve as bollards.

In 1992, English Heritage shipped-in five 18th-century cannons to the Garrison – two 6-pounders, two 12-pounders and one iron muzzle-loading gun capable of firing a cannonball up to 3,000 yards, this latter installed on the 1793 emplacement at King Charles's Battery.

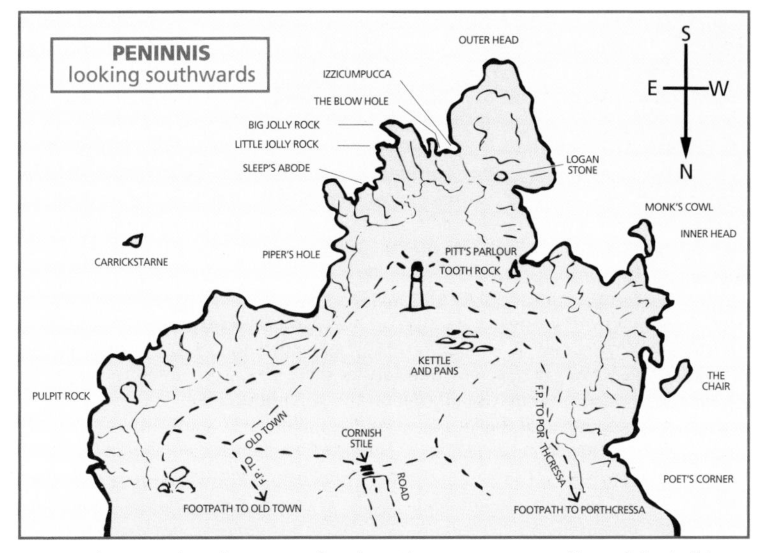

From the coastal road one can often hear the monotonous tolling of the bell-buoy which marks the Spanish Ledges. The road passes the old Trinity House Cottages where the lighthouse keepers' families used to live, but no longer do so as all lighthouses are now automatic. Then the lane passes the secluded royal bungalow, Tamarisk, and the Duchy of Cornwall offices, and finally arrives back at the Garrison Gate, near which can be seen the old cell for the detention of petty wrong-doers.

The Peninnis Walk

The parish church is the Church of St. Mary the Virgin (built 1835–7) and has seating arrangements similar to those in the chapel of an Oxbridge college. There are some stained-glass windows by Kempe, an 1866 Willis Hall organ, and, in the forecourt, two 1727 Board of Ordnance lead water tanks. For the Peninnis Walk, take the road from the church up the hill past the Chaplaincy, and turn sharp right just before reaching the brow of the hill. Fifty yards along this road, there is a fork; the right fork leads to St. Mary's Hospital, built in 1938, and to **Buzza Tower**, an old windmill, named after a local farmer, fitted with seats to commemorate the visit of Edward VII in 1902 – a fine spot to watch a sunset. The left fork leads to the pagoda-shaped Health Centre – which has geothermal heating – and to Peninnis, accessible over a Cornish stile near the foundations of an old mill, beside which there used to be the cottage where lived Scilly's 'primitive' poet, Robert Maybee.

Peninnis is a rugged promontory on which several ships have been wrecked. When the *Minnehaha*, a large four-masted vessel, struck on Peninnis in 1874, half the crew of eighteen saved themselves by clambering along the bowsprit and jumping on to the rocks. In 1963 the ship's bell was salvaged intact from the seabed and is now in the superb local museum in Church Street.

The other route to Peninnis is along the coastal footpath from Porthcressa which eventually leads to the Inner Head (see map). The curved crest or tuft on the summit of the outermost point is known as the **Monk's Cowl** from a fancied resemblance to a hooded head. The path eventually reaches the perpendicular **Tooth Rock**, inland from which on the grass incline are the **Kettle and Pans**, rocks so named from the large rock basins worn to a rounded shape by rainwater.

In the labyrinth of rocks below the lighthouse is the 300 ton **Logan Stone** which at one time rocked quite easily, matches and even coins being bent by inserting them in a crevice under the rock on the west side and pushing from the other side. The balance is said to have been upset by German bombs dropped on Peninnis in the Second World War and, despite attempts to right it, the stone no longer rocks easily. Also situated south of the lighthouse is **Big Jolly Rock**, a large area of flat-topped rock scarred with deep crevices. On its west side is a narrow gully where waves rush in to disappear under a wedged boulder, and emerge under pressure through a small aperture known as the **Blow-hole**, cascading in white foam over the rocks beyond. About twelve yards to the west is a cavern with the intriguing name of **Izzicumpucca**, but the only real cave on Peninnis is **Piper's Hole** to the east of Big Jolly Rock. It is rich with legends, but is not more than fifty feet long and has a much longer namesake on Tresco.

East of Piper's Hole is the unmistakable **Pulpit Rock**, a forty-seven foot projection resembling the sounding board of a pulpit, which appears at a distance to be imperfectly supported and threatening to topple at any moment, but is actually quite secure. From this rock, if one looks back towards the lighthouse, several overlapping rocks can be seen forming the effigy of a **Witch's Head**. Diligent seekers can also find effigies of the **Tuskless Elephant**, the **Laughing Old Man**, the **Sleeping Bear**, the **Walrus** and many other fancifully-named granite rocks, all within about 100 metres of the lighthouse.

Old Town

From the Pulpit Rock there is a path around the coast to Old Town Church, which is a fragment of a large cruciform church dating back to the twelfth century. Services are held regularly in the church. Against the wall of Old Town churchyard, to the right of one of the two gates leading to Old Town Bay, is the grave of the naval surgeon Abraham Leggatt who, at his own instructions, was buried upright in 1809 in a strong granite coffin that doubles as his headstone. Inscribed on the stone is the inspiring inscription: 'He pray'd daily that God would make him instrumental in his hands to ease the pains and remove the complaints of the afflicted. Brethren, do likewise and may the Lord deliver us!' Curiously (or perhaps carelessly) the mason has inscribed one word twice.

Old Town churchyard contains the graves of many members of old Scillonian families, of some service personnel of the Second World War, and also of some of the 335 passengers whose lives were lost when the liner *Schiller* was wrecked on the Western Rocks in 1875. The huge granite obelisk on the highest point in the churchyard is to Louise Holzmaister, the pretty, 23-year-old newly-wed, who was travelling in the *Schiller* from the USA to join her millionaire husband in Germany, but whose body was never found. On 6th June, 1995, Lord Wilson was buried here, and among the hundreds of mourners who walked behind the coffin from the church in

Hugh Town were Lord Callaghan, Tony Blair, and a well-known Scillonian, Richard Lethbridge, who died the next day.

The path follows the sea wall towards Old Town, above which, covered with mesembryanthemum, is Castle Ennor which, in the Middle Ages, was the main defence on St. Mary's. No ruins of the castle remain as many of the castle's stones have been taken for building projects elsewhere, but it is still possible to climb the eminence for the view. Nearby is the Old Town Café which serves meals, including traditional cream teas. In the lane alongside the café is the start of the **Nature Trail** through the Lower Moors.

Old Town has a delightful beach for children, sheltered and facing south. At low water a shallow, sandy pool is formed, protected from the open sea by banks of seaweed. Off the road leading south to Tolman Point, is the Tolman Café, and a large tank carved from one block of granite, which in former times was used for salting pilchards but was originally a coffin.

The Porth Hellick Walk

Take the road past the lifeboat slip and then the turning to the right past Parting Carn (see map) and eventually (by turning right again at the second turning) to Salakee and the beach at Porth Hellick, which is rich in seashells. At the eastern corner of the bay is the rough monument to Sir Cloudesley Shovell. A **Nature Trail** starts near here.

On a promontory west of Porth Hellick is an early cliff castle known as **Giant's Castle**. To the east are some overhanging rocks called the **Clapper Rocks**, and others known as the **Loaded Camel** and the **Archdruid's Chair**. Nearby is **Porth Hellick Down Burial Chamber**, a 4,000 years old entrance-grave, which is maintained by English Heritage. There are obvious signs of five others in the area which are not maintained.

The coastal footpath continues past Deep Point and eventually curves round to **Pelistry Bay**, where there is one of Scilly's favourite beaches, certainly with St. Mary's islanders on summer weekends. Here there is a sand bar over to **Toll's Island**, where there are several kelp pits and also remains of **Pellew's Redoubt**, a late 18th century battery named after and constructed by Captain Edward Pellew, commandant in Scilly, to protect the eastern side of St. Mary's from possible French attack. Pellew was brought up in Hawk's Farm, Alverton Road, Penzance, and became one of Britain's greatest admirals, being created Viscount Exmouth in 1816.

From Pelistry a road leads back to Hugh Town via **Holy Vale** (believed to have been the site of a convent or monastic cell) and Rocky Hill.

The Telegraph Walk

Take the road past the lifeboat slip and then the footpath along the shore by **Porthmellon** (see map). This path skirts Porth Thomas (Shark's Pit), above which are the uncompleted, 16th-century fortifications known as **Harry's Walls**, and eventually joins the road at Porthloo leading up to the golf course. Before reaching the golf course, St. Mary's circular coastal path branches off to the left, and a short way along this path is Juliet's Garden Restaurant. Beyond the golf course, on the highest point on the islands, where the mainland is visible on clear days, is **Telegraph Tower**, a Grade 2 listed building. Here, in 1898, Marconi received what was then the longest-ever transmarine wireless signal (from Porthcurno), and, in 1903, he showed Edward VII around the station.

— TRESCO —

ENGLAND'S ISLAND OF FLOWERS

www.tresco.co.uk

TRESCO is one of the world's most beautiful islands, lying in sheltered, brilliantly-coloured, crystal-clear water at the heart of the Isles of Scilly. Here are the world-famous Botanical Gardens with rare, sub-tropical plants and trees, and the Valhalla Maritime Museum of Ships' Figureheads. Open daily, Tresco has everything to offer for a perfect holiday, and a variety of accommodation to suit all tastes.

AA RAC

THE ISLAND HOTEL

BTA Recommended

The Island Hotel is well-known for its comfort, friendly service and excellent cuisine. Situated by the sea, with private beach, secluded garden, tennis court and outdoor swimming pool, it has 48 bedrooms – all with private bathrooms – also one suite.

The spacious Terrace Bar is open to non-residents for morning coffee, sandwiches, lunches and cream teas.

Brochure, tariff, and details of Special Gardeners' Holidays are available on application to the Manager. Telephone: Scillonia (01720) 422883

AA★★

THE NEW INN

Near the small harbour of New Grimsby on Tresco is a centuries-old inn, which is open all year round. All twin/double rooms have private bathrooms, central heating, TV and tea-making facilities. The restaurant specialises in locally-caught seafood, whilst the bars – which are open all day from April to September – offer a full range of bar food which can be enjoyed in the bar or gardens.

~ CHRISTMAS AND WINTER BREAKS AVAILABLE ~

Please write or phone for a brochure and tariff.

Telephone: Scillonia (01720) 422844

HOLIDAY COTTAGES

Attractive traditional cottages, luxuriously appointed, are available throughout the year to sleep from 2 to 10 persons.

For further details and a colour brochure, please contact:
TRESCO ESTATE OFFICE, Tresco, Isles of Scilly, TR24 0QQ
Telephone: Scillonia (01720) 422849/422566

There are mounted binoculars at the top of the Tower, originally from Hitler's Atlantic Wall; but the post is no longer permanently manned by the coastguards, since radio communication has largely replaced visual watch. The aerials at Telegraph represent radio, television and telephone services.

A lane running north from Telegraph leads near Bant's Carn Burial Chamber of about 1,800 BC, and the excavations of a village which was occupied from about 200 BC to about AD 300 (and which in 1999 was found to be more extensive) to Bar Point (see map). A sand bar stretches from near here to Tresco and to St. Martin's, and a sea wall or causeway once existed on its top. Only at high tide is there sufficient depth of water over the bar for *Scillonian III* to take this shorter route to and from Penzance. The path eastwards from Bar Point leads to two Bronze Age burial chambers at **Innisidgen**, and eventually to **Watermill Cove** and **Pelistry**.

A visit to the **Longstone Heritage Centre** in the centre of St. Mary's (see map) is recommended, and it contains also a restaurant and garden shop. Nearby is the project known as **Carreg Dhu** (Black Rock), a voluntary enterprise by islanders and visitors begun in 1986 to turn an old quarry into a 1½ acre sub-tropical community garden, whose name has a local pronunciation sounding something like 'Crake Dew'.

TRESCO

In the 12th century a priory to St. Nicholas was founded on Tresco by Benedictine monks, but little remains of any buildings today apart from some walling and two archways. Around it are the sub-tropical gardens begun by Augustus Smith, who was granted a lease of all Scilly by the Duchy of Cornwall in 1834 and built the Abbey as his home. He never married, but insisted his nephew and heir, Algernon Smith-Dorrien, add the name 'Smith' before inheriting the lease, the family afterwards dropping the first 'Smith' except on legal documents. Major Arthur Dorrien Smith succeeded in 1918 and was in turn succeeded by Lt. Cmdr. Tom Dorrien Smith, the only surviving son of four who served in the armed services in the Second World War. Robert Dorrien Smith succeeded as leasee in 1973, by which time only Tresco was part of the lease.

Each member of the family has enlarged the gardens and added to its exotic flora. The gardens are never a mass of colour like many parks, but have something to offer of interest in every month, Walter Besant describing it as 'Kew with the roof off'. It contains plants which do not grow well in the open anywhere else in Britain, an achievement made possible by the equable climate. Among the plants are Citrons, Bananas, Mexican Yuccas, Chilean Puya, New Zealand Ironwood, Burmese Honeysuckle, Himalayan Ginger, Australian Scarlet Bottle-brush, Madeira Lily-of-the-Valley trees, Aloes, Dracaenas, Indian Fan Palms, Chinese Paper Plants, Prickly Pears, Mimosa, Cinnamon, Musk and gigantic Ice-plants.

The red-flowered *Xeronema callistemon* flowered in the open here in 1999 for the first time in Britain, and the world's fastest-growing flowering plant, the *Liliaceae hesperogucca whipplei* – which flowers only once in about twenty years – set the world record in 1978 by growing twelve feet in fourteen days on the Middle Terrace, according to the Guinness Book of Records (1998).

Among features to look for in the garden are the bronze carving by David Wynne of the three eldest children of Robert Dorrien Smith at the bottom of the Lighthouse

DIAGRAM ILLUSTRATING THE PRINCIPAL PATHS IN TRESCO ABBEY GARDENS

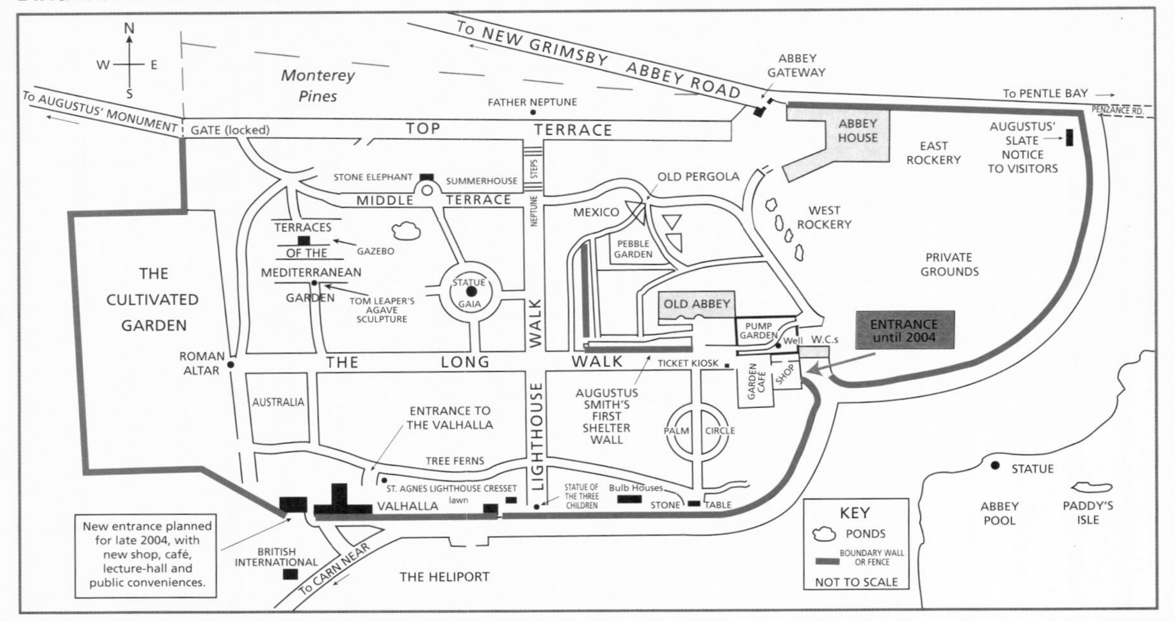

Cornwall is notable for its many fine gardens open to the public, particularly those in the valleys with streams running south into the English Channel, such as the National Trust's Glendurgan. But none can quite match Tresco Abbey which, among its other interesting features – and made possible only by the relatively equable nature of Scilly's climate – is its exceptionally wide variety of plants growing in the open close together, but many originating from altogether different climes.

The roofless garden marked 'Old Abbey' in the diagram is the site of the former priory dating from the 12th century but probably deserted even before Henry VIII's Dissolution of the Monasteries in 1536 and 1539. The building was probably destroyed by fire when Admiral Blake invaded Tresco and defeated the rebellious Cavaliers in 1651. After the 17th century the site was used as a cemetery by Tresco islanders until the churchyard was constructed. On a stone under the smaller of the building's archways is the oldest writing found in Scilly.

Walk (see map), Wynne's statue of Gaia, the Earth-mother of Greek Mythology, sculpted in 1989 from African Marble (Prince Charles has a copy at Highgrove), and in the Gazebo in the Mediterranean Garden, a shell decoration by Lucy Dorrien Smith which is an artistic creation of simple yet staggering beauty. Also, off the garden, is the Valhalla containing figureheads, cannon and other items from shipwrecks, and, at the western end of the Long Walk, an altar of Roman times from St. Mary's.

The garden is open every day (10.00–16.00 with an admission charge) and has a shop and a café. Tresco has no cars, but there are farm vehicles and golf buggies – and also many bicycles which can be hired by visitors staying at the Island Hotel, New Inn or in timeshare cottages. Landings are made at Carn Near (see map), or at New Grimsby, where there is a shop, café and public conveniences. Dogs must be kept on the lead. From New Grimsby a path leads northwards past the rough-hewn secret steps of the Special Operations Executive (in 1943 they controlled up to 1,500 agents in German-occupied Europe) to Cromwell's Castle, a round tower, sixty feet high, completed in 1651 prior to the first of three wars against the Dutch. In the channel opposite is Hangman Island (*An Main* which, to an English visitor, may sound something like 'hangman', but is actually Old Cornish for 'the island' and has no connection with capital punishment. There is no record of anyone being executed on the island). On the hill above Cromwell's Castle is King Charles' Castle, built 1550–4, which Cromwell's Castle superseded because the guns of the earlier fort could not depress satisfactorily to command Tresco Channel.

From King Charles's Castle, **Piper's Hole** can be found by walking across the down (on which a number of early tin workings can be detected) in the direction of Round Island lighthouse. On reaching the cliff, turn westwards and follow the cliff edge until a gully can be seen leading from the sea.

Piper's Hole is a legendary haunt of smugglers and, more whimsically, the home of mermaids. It is an interesting cave which penetrates underground for about eighty metres. The entrance is unpretentious, but after one has clambered a few yards over slippery boulders, the cave abruptly opens out and there is a freshwater pool about ten metres across. If candles are placed on convenient ledges around the chamber, their reflection on the shimmering water turns the cave into a fairyland. Across the pool there is a shingle floor, the cave continuing through a series of rocky arches and high vaulted chambers for nearly twenty paces. An enterprising islander kept a punt on the lake for many years to ferry people across the pool for a small fee, but the craft has long since broken up, so an inflatable raft – together with torches – will be found useful equipment on an expedition to explore this intriguing cave. Among many visitors who have been delighted by the cave was Dame Ethel Smyth, the pioneer suffragist and the United Kingdom's greatest woman composer, whose opera *The Wreckers* (1903) has a scene which was inspired by her exploration of Piper's Hole in 1886.

From New Grimsby the road leads past the New Inn, then over the hill and past some timeshare holiday homes, to the church of St. Nicholas and the island school at Old Grimsby on the east coast. The Island Hotel is situated nearby in a superb setting close to its private beach of Raven's Porth. To the south is the **Old Blockhouse**, built in the 16th century. In 1651, Robert Blake with a force of Roundheads successfully invaded Tresco at this point from Teän and defeated the rebel Cavaliers.

Tresco Abbey Gardens. *Photo: Keith Dibley*

At Tresco Heliport, just south of the Abbey Gardens, are flights from and to Penzance. In 2003, Bronze Age huts, connected by passageways and possibly over 3,000 years old, were found below Tresco heliport and cricket pitch.

ST. MARTIN'S

St. Martin's is noted for its long sandy beaches, from which the bathing is excellent, and for the remarkable vividness of its colourings.

Visitors are usually landed at Higher Town Quay in the bay below Higher Town (see map) but, owing to the shallowness of the sea at low water, a longish pull in a punt (local name for row-boat) may be necessary at very low tides. Alternatively, landings can be made at the quay at Lower Town, near the hotel.

Public conveniences are situated at Higher Town Quay in a building on the bank immediately above the beach. A narrow, concrete road leads from here up the hill to Higher Town – where are the Polreath Tea Rooms, post-office stores and the Sailing Centre – through Middle Town, and on to Lower Town, where are the Seven Stones Inn and the hotel. To the east are the **Day Mark** – built in 1683 (not in 1637 as inscribed) as a guide to shipping and still serving this purpose – and some interesting-looking entrances to caves which prove disappointingly short on entry, of which the largest are **Pope's Hole** and **Culver Hole**. To the north-west is White Island, accessible across the boulders at half tide. There is a cave called **Underland Girt** with a forbidding entrance at the end of an inlet on the eastern side of White Island, and, nearby, a deep fissure called **Chad Girt**. White Island overlooks the wide sweep of **Great Bay** on St. Martin's, at higher tides one of Scilly's finest beaches. On White Island, above Porth Morran, several kelp pits can be detected, where seaweed used to be burnt to extract the soda, which was then exported to Bristol and Gloucester for use in making soap, alum and glass.

Inland from Higher Town Bay is Little Arthur Café and Farm, this latter an area of eight acres run on ecological and self-sufficiency principles. A trail open to the public runs through the farm with notices to guide and explain.

A twenty-four bedroom, single-storey, luxury hotel was opened in 1989 and is situated on a superb site at Lower Town. It blends well with the landscape and is designed to resemble a row of cottages.

In 1989, a granite statue, believed to be over 3,000 years old – and therefore one of the oldest in Britain – was rediscovered on Chapel Down and re-erected. It is a carving of a human face on top of a pillar, but the features are hard to distinguish now. In the same year, a small horseshoe-shaped bracelet was found washed ashore on a beach on St. Martin's. The British Museum declared that it was of gold and also about 3,000 years old.

Two businesses on St. Martin's won national awards in 2003 – the Bakery and *Scented Island Flowers by Post* (see page 58).

ST. AGNES AND THE GUGH

From St. Mary's, launches approach St. Agnes by way of St. Mary's Sound, where the tidal current is strong, past the **Kittern** (see map) which, when viewed from a launch approaching Porth Conger, shows a remarkable likeness to the imposing profile of Queen Victoria. Passing between the Gugh and the Cow (avoiding the Calf, a tapering pinnacle of rock submerged at high tide in a dangerous position near the middle of the channel), the launch enters **Porth Conger** where there are the quay, the Turk's Head public house, and public conveniences. A narrow concrete road runs from the quay over the back of the island. If one follows it up the hill, a track leading off to the left gives access to the sand bar between Porth Conger and **The Cove**. Visitors may cross over the sand bar but should take care not to be stranded when the tide is flowing. Porth Conger and The Cove have excellent beaches from which to bathe, but it is dangerous to do so when the sea covers the bar. The two houses on the Gugh have curved roofs specially designed to deflect gales.

On the Gugh is an isolated, nine foot high, standing stone, **The Old Man of Gugh**, one of a number of such stones in Scilly which are believed to have been associated with rituals in the Bronze Age. On Kittern Hill are several ancient burial places, including one called **Obadiah's Barrow,** which was excavated in 1900 by George Bonsor, and found to contain a sitting skeleton together with a dozen urns containing cremated human remains. One of these urns can be seen in the Museum on St. Mary's.

On St. Agnes the concrete path leads westwards across the island, past the café at Covean Cottage and the Post-Office-Stores, to a junction. Near here is the white tower of St. Agnes lighthouse, which shone for 231 years, a fire burning in its cresset until 1790 when Argand lamps were fitted: the right fork here leads to **Big Pool**, a favourite spot for ornithologists to observe passage migrants, and to **Periglis** where are the old lifeboat slips – the longest in Britain – and the church (built in 1827).The last four bodies recovered from the wreck of the liner *Schiller* are buried in the churchyard, but many bodies from the wreck were never found. The left fork leads past the old coastguard cottages to the open down, where there is a remarkably-weathered rock called the **Nag's Head**. The trail westwards is conveniently marked by clear but unobtrusive white-painted, double-lines, and leads to **Troy Town Maze**, which is a labyrinth of small stones arranged by a lighthouse keeper in 1729 from a much earlier maze believed to have been on the same site. Walking its path is said to promote wellbeing, but others believe that it is principally the beneficial effects of a holiday in

Scilly, rather than walking the maze, which account for the subsequent feelings of contentment which some visitors claim to experience. The coastal trail southwards from here leads past **St. Warna's Well** to rocky **St. Warna's Cove**, where legend says the patron saint of shipwrecks landed from Ireland in her wicker coracle, but which hardly looks a suitable place for uncanonised persons to attempt a landing. The trail continues over **Wingletang Down** near the **Punch Bowl** (a large rock with a deep basin in the top, poised uncertainly on another rock) to **Beady Pool**, where brown and black-and-white beads of seventeenth-century Dutch manufacture can still occasionally be found washed ashore from the old wreck of a merchant ship. Some of these beads can be seen in the Museum on St. Mary's. In 1878 the population of St. Agnes was estimated to be nearly 150 arranged in twenty-five households, of whom the heads of seventeen were surnamed Hicks, and this is still a common surname on the island.

BRYHER

From the short Church Quay (near which are public conveniences), a lane winds up the hill past All Saints' Church – which has interesting lanterns – to a fork: the left fork leads to Hell Bay Hotel and the Great Pool – a site for birdwatchers – and to a delightful sandy beach at Rushy Bay, notable for its excellent bathing and interesting shells along the tide lines; the right fork leads to Vine House Tea-rooms and eventually down to the post office at Bryher Stores, Fraggle Rock Restaurant at Norrard, and to Bryher's camp site. From here a path northwards is indicated at occasional intervals by waymarkers (two parallel white lines painted on a stone), and leads to aptly-named Hell Bay – see map. When a big sea is running, Atlantic rollers break on the shore here with full force, creating a swirling spume of spray.

Beyond Hell Bay is an old cliff castle at Shipman Head where birds nest between March and July, but are best left undisturbed. On returning from Hell Bay, it is worth climbing the summit of Watch Hill, which has an old lookout post where the panoramic view is considered one of the best in Scilly. In 1999, a farm tractor's wheel fell into an unsuspected burial cist, in which was a 2,000-year-old metal sword, thirty-four inches long and still in its scabbard. Among other items in the grave and now in St. Mary's Museum was an oval, bronze mirror of similar age.

Bryher also has one of the longest caves in Scilly – High Rock Cave – but it is hard to find and even harder to enter, for the sea runs into its entrance; this is about thirty feet high, but with a width of only about four feet. Flotsam and jetsam are sometimes washed into its recesses, but visitors are warned of the danger of attempting to enter except at low water on a spring tide in a dead calm sea and with plenty of back-up.

THE EASTERN ISLANDS

Landings on St. Martin's are often made after a round trip of the Eastern Islands to see some of the wildlife or to land some visitors on an uninhabited island to enjoy it to themselves for a few hours. **Little Arthur** (pronounced 'Arter' locally) has a sandy beach, and it is a short walk to **Great Arthur** where there are some prehistoric graves; on this island's western slopes are signs of other burials, one of which – it is speculatively suggested – could be the grave of King Arthur, conveyed to Avalon (Scilly?) after being mortally wounded at the Battle of Camlann in about AD 537.

If you 'want to be alone' in Scilly, **Great Ganilly** is the largest of the Eastern Islands and a pleasant spot to indulge Crusoe-inspired fantasies of ruling a deserted island. It is infrequently visited, but not because of the winning limerick in the 1959 W.I. competition:

There was an old lady of Scilly
Who found it too hot on Ganilly;
She sat in a pool
To try to keep cool,
In the end she felt frightfully chilly.

– with apologies to Edward Lear and LMD.

ST. HELEN'S AND TEÄN

On St. Helen's there are the remains of a 10th-century oratory, to which there is an annual pilgrimage at the beginning of August, and of ancient huts excavated 1956–58. The most obvious ruin is the 3-roomed, granite and brick pest-house built in the 18th century for isolating people from passing ships suspected of carrying the plague, although never used for this purpose. Adjacent to St. Helen's is the friendly island of Teän, which was inhabited in 1684 by the Nance family from Falmouth who made a living mainly by kelping. Landings are possible at any tide. It is likely that St. Helen's and Teän first became islands with the rising of the sea, possibly in the 11th century. The dieresis over the 'a' is of some importance, indicating that the pronunciation of Teän in Scilly is in two syllables as in naïve and Brontë.

NATURE CONSERVATION

In order to foster nature conservation most of the heathland and wet areas of Scilly, together with most of the uninhabited islands, have been designated as Sites of Special Scientific Interest by English Nature. To help safeguard birds the following restrictions are in force:

Islands open all the year round include

Some Eastern Isles, Guther's Island, Gweal, Northwethel, Puffin Island, St. Helen's, Samson, Teän, White Island (off Samson), and White Island (off St. Martin's).

Islands closed 15th March to 20th August, except by permit

Western Rocks (including Gorregan, The Daisy, Rosevear, Rosevean, and Great and Little Crebawethan), Melledgan, Annet, Norrard Rocks (including Mincarlo, Castle Bryher, Illiswilgig, Maiden Bower and Scilly Rock), Green Island (off Samson), Stony Island, Men-a-vaur, Menawethan, Great and Little Innisvouls, and southern end of Great Ganilly. Persons engaged in genuine research of benefit to nature conservation may apply for permission to visit these islands by writing to The Isles of Scilly Wildlife Trust, St. Mary's, Isles of Scilly.

Visitors are reminded that it is an offence to take or destroy the eggs of wild birds; it may also be injudicious and even dangerous to walk into the bird colonies. For instance, on the southern slopes of Gugh and Samson, gulls can become most upset and dive threateningly upon intruders even as late as August. Everyone is asked, therefore, to try not to disturb bird life, and also to assist in helping to preserve the natural environment.

EDUCATION IN SCILLY

Until 2001, there were four primary schools (on St. Mary's, Tresco, St. Martin's and St. Agnes), and one secondary school at Carn Thomas on St. Mary's which provided mixed comprehensive secondary education to the school-leaving age. Falling school rolls, the experiment since 1997 of a combined head for St. Mary's secondary and primary schools, and the urgent hope of economies, led to the decision in 2002 to have one headteacher and one governing body for all five schools in Scilly. This is the first LEA school in the UK to be federated, catering for ages 5 to 16 in five 'bases'.

About two dozen off-island children of secondary-school age continue to attend the secondary school, staying in term-time as weekly-boarders in the school boarding-house in Church Street. Tresco School's pupil numbers are around 20 for they include the primary-age children of Bryher, who cross by boat to Tresco each day and enjoy lunch in the New Inn. The pupils in St. Mary's primary school number nearly 100, while those in St. Mary's secondary school are about 110; but the pupils at either St. Martin's school or St. Agnes school have for years rarely reached double figures.

This educational provision is impressive. The pupil–teacher ratio is good, and the children are much stimulated by their environment and are noticeably self-reliant and friendly. Some indication of educational standards in Scilly today is provided in the tables of exam results. In 2003 87.5% of GCSE candidates of the Isles of Scilly education authority (the smallest LEA in the UK with only one school) achieved grades A to C in five or more subjects, their highest percentage yet. The school is administered by the local education authority, which consists of all twenty-one councillors (who sit as independents without party labels) and four co-opted members. Education became, in effect, compulsory in Scilly thirty years before it became law in the rest of the UK, because the far-seeing Augustus John Smith, Lord Proprietor from 1834 to 1872, built schools on all the main islands and insisted on children attending, imposing a fine on parents who failed to send them.

AREA AND POPULATION	Area		Population		
	in Acres	in Hectares	*(1822)	(1831)	**(1991)
St. Mary's	1,554	629	1,400	1,278	1,590
Tresco	735	297	480	465	165
St. Martin's and White Island	586	237	280	235	110
St. Agnes and the Gugh	366	148	282	244	90
Bryher and Gweal	327	133	140	111	75
Samson	95	39	34	32	nil
Annet	53	21	nil	nil	nil
St. Helen's	49	20	nil	nil	nil
Teän	40	16	nil	nil	nil
Great Gannilly	33	13	nil	nil	nil
Other islands	125	51	nil	nil	nil
Isles of Scilly (TOTALS)	3,963	1,604	2,616	2,365	2,030

** as estimated by Woodley*

*** adjusted census count*

CAMPING ON SCILLY

The only camping permitted on the islands is on authorised camp sites. These are:

St. Mary's – Mrs. B. Moulson, Garrison Farm. (Tel: 01720 422670)

St. Agnes – Mrs. S. J. Hicks, Troy Town Farm. (Tel: 01720 422360)

St. Martin's – Mrs. C. Savill, Middle Town. (Tel: 01720 422888)

Bryher – Mrs. K. Stedeford, Jenford. (Tel: 01720 422886)

The number of campers on any one site is restricted; it is therefore prudent to make a prior booking. The four sites are family-run and on the level, with hot showers and flush toilets, but open fires are not permitted on the islands. Caravans and motor-caravans are not allowed to be shipped to the islands, and visitors' cars are unnecessary for active holidaymakers.

SCOUTS AND GUIDES

Scouts should apply to: Mr. E. Jowett, County Assistant Secretary of Cornwall Scout Council, New Carlyon, Carclaze, St. Austell, Cornwall, PL25 4EL. Tel: 01726 63396.

Guides should apply to: Mrs. M. Eddy, Cornwall Activity Advisor, Mare Laree, Cove Road, Sennen, Penzance, TR19 7BT. Tel: 01736 871252.

SAMSON

Samson, with its two hills joined by a sandy isthmus, is a landmark for visitors who soon become familiar with its contours. Stone walls surrounding former fields, which over past centuries have been inundated by a rising sea, can still be discerned at low water on the sandy flats east of Samson. They served as fish traps for the needy inhabitants until 1855, when Augustus Smith evacuated the last household whose members had grown too old to support themselves. The population has fluctuated; Borlase mentions two families in 1752 living on South Hill, which increased to thirty-three people in nine houses by 1833 – but today all the buildings are in ruins. However, Holy Farm, Edward Webber's house – everyone was surnamed Webber or Woodcock – which is halfway up the slope of South Hill on the west side, has come to be regarded, by tradition, as the home of Armorel, the heroine of Sir Walter Besant's novel *Armorel of Lyonesse*.

On North Hill is a kistvaen, or sepulchral stone-box, of special interest as the stones have been fashioned to fit into each other by means of grooves. On the south-west slopes of South Hill, Lesser Black-backed Gulls nest in large numbers.

ANNET AND THE WESTERN ROCKS

Annet is a bird sanctuary and landing is restricted. The island is honeycombed with Puffin and Shearwater burrows under the very extensive Sea Thrift. Just after the breeding season the island is often a sorrowful sight, for large numbers of the young birds perish, mostly due to the depredations of the Great Black-backed Gull. Beyond Annet are the Western Rocks, the outposts of the archipelago and the graveyard of many ships. Some bear fitting names such as the Crim, the Dogs of Scilly, Crebinicks, and Hellweathers, while others seem quite inappropriate such as Rosevear, Rosevean and the Daisy!

On Rosevear, on which grow fewer than half a dozen varieties of vegetation, are the ruins of stone huts built by the men who constructed the Bishop Rock lighthouse. In spring, birds nest all over the island; in autumn, the island turns into a nursery for seal pups.

FLOWERS

The flower industry in Scilly dates from 1868 when William Trevellick of Rocky Hill Farm first sent some cut-flowers to Covent Garden packed in a hatbox. He received £1, after which the industry grew rapidly until today daffodils and narcissi are the islands' glory as well as providing the inhabitants with a winter livelihood.

The mild Scillonian winter enables flowers to be grown in the open and gives farmers in Scilly a few weeks' start in harvesting the flowers over many of their mainland rivals. Daffodils and narcissi are picked in the bud and then packed in boxes to be sent by air or sea to markets in the UK, Germany, Scandinavia. The aim is for the flowers to arrive in perfect condition but not fully developed.

The picking season starts with *Paper Whites* in October and lasts up to six months, ending with *Cheerfulness, Actea* and *Golden Dawn* as late as April. The *Soleil d'Or* (golden sun) is the principal crop; it has a delightful bi-coloured flower and a strong scent, and it does not thrive anywhere in Britain as well as it does in Scilly. Other varieties follow, such as *Scilly White, Primo, Avalanche, Grand Monarch* and trumpet varieties such as *King Alfred* and *Fortune*, but there are still plenty of flowers left in the fields in March and April to provide visitors with a riot of colour.

To help induce the bulbs to flower early, polythene sheets are often placed over the fields for a few weeks in spring and early summer. Some farmers use tractors carrying cylinders of propane gas to heat the soil and so produce a similar result. Each year from June, many of the bulbs are dug up in rotation and treated for eelworm by soaking them for a few hours in hot water with a dash of formalin – for efficacy the temperature is critical – such treatment and replanting continuing for most of the summer. Polythene sheets placed on the flower fields from August are there to retard flower growth, so extending the season. In an average year, over four hundred tons of flowers (including the boxes) may be exported (a quarter of these grown on the off-islands), and this amounts to about thirty million blooms. Fortunately, flower farming neatly complements tourism, for it provides work throughout the winter.

By 2002, flower farming accounted for less than fifteen per cent of Scilly's income, with tourism making up most of the rest. Yet the forty-five or so farmers in Scilly continue to thrive and to develop new varieties, although they face competition from growers nearer the markets, and from unseasonal flowers flown to Britain from other parts of the world; moreover, public taste in flowers varies unpredictably and prices fluctuate widely.

Besides the flowers grown commercially in the small flower fields, there is an abundance of wild flowers throughout the year; especially prominent are pink **Sea Thrift** and **Mesembryanthemum** – otherwise known in some variants as Hottentot Fig because the nomadic tribesmen of South-West Africa, where the plant originated, used to eat its fleshy fruit.

The pleasures of sunning oneself on an isolated rock among the Eastern Islands on a summer afternoon are not going to be spoilt by an intrusive launch crowded with humans taking photographs. Haven't they seen a pregnant Atlantic Grey Seal before? (At birth the pup will weigh about 12 kilos). *Photo: David Rogers*

A pair of Puffins (Sea Parrots). They come to land in April to nest in burrows on Annet, but after July leave to spend the rest of the year far out at sea. *Photo: Gibson, Scilly*

Some wild flowers such as **Dwarf Pansy** and **Early Adder's Tongue** grow nowhere else in Britain in the open, while many former crops, such as **Ixias** and **Whistling Jacks** (a form of gladiola so-called because the leaves whistle when placed between the palms and blown through) are farm escapes and now grow in colourful profusion among the 700 or so wild flowers of Scilly, the wide variety of which makes the islands botanically interesting.

CLIMATE

The Isles of Scilly enjoy an equable climate with small variation between day and night temperatures. The range of monthly mean temperatures over the year is 9°C as compared with 14°C at Kensington Palace, London. Scilly has a higher January mean temperature (8°C) than Cannes, and the average of the minimum night temperatures in January is the same as that at Kensington Palace in late April. It may therefore be claimed that Scilly is as warm in winter as the Mediterranean Riviera, and that winter nights in Scilly are as warm as spring nights in London.

Scilly has more sunshine during the year than most mainland resorts, May and June being particularly sunny. In normal winters air frost and snow are absent, and (rather rashly) the islanders have claimed to have only two seasons, spring and summer. In summer, the air rarely becomes sultry because there is usually a breeze off the sea on a sunny day. Rainfall is not excessive and thunderstorms are rarely severe. Winds, however, can be high, and account for the belts of fir trees being planted across St. Mary's and Tresco, and also for the tall hedges of *Euonymus* from Japan, *Hedge Veronica* from South Island, New Zealand, *Pittosporum crassifolium* from North Island, New Zealand, *Escallonia macrantha* from the island of Chiloe, discovered by Spaniards off the coast of Chile in 1558, and *Oleania repens*, also from New Zealand, among some others. These are all plants that thrive in salty air and have strong, evergreen leaves and well-developed roots capable of withstanding high winds – most suitable to surround the small fields and shelter the early flowers.

It is said of the climate of the Isles of Scilly that visitors in the summer who are unfortunate enough to encounter a bad spell can console themselves with the thought that, however inclement the weather may be, it is usually worse on the mainland of England (see page 68).

TIDES

At spring tides, which roughly coincide with the new moon and full moon, the difference between low and high water in Scilly may be over sixteen feet. At neap tides, the difference may be only eight feet. The times of high tide are chalked up each day on a board on St. Mary's Quay. Very approximately, the tide flows for six hours and then ebbs for the next six hours. On most beaches bathing is at its best when the tide is near high water, whereas shrimping and searching for crabs, sea anemones, and sea-urchins are best at low water. At spring low tides it is possible to walk from Tresco to Bryher and Samson, and considerable distances can be walked on dry sand from St. Martin's over the flats towards Tresco and St. Mary's. But visitors are advised against attempting these feats without an accompanying boat, as miscalculation of the time of the tide change could result in their being cut off by the incoming sea.

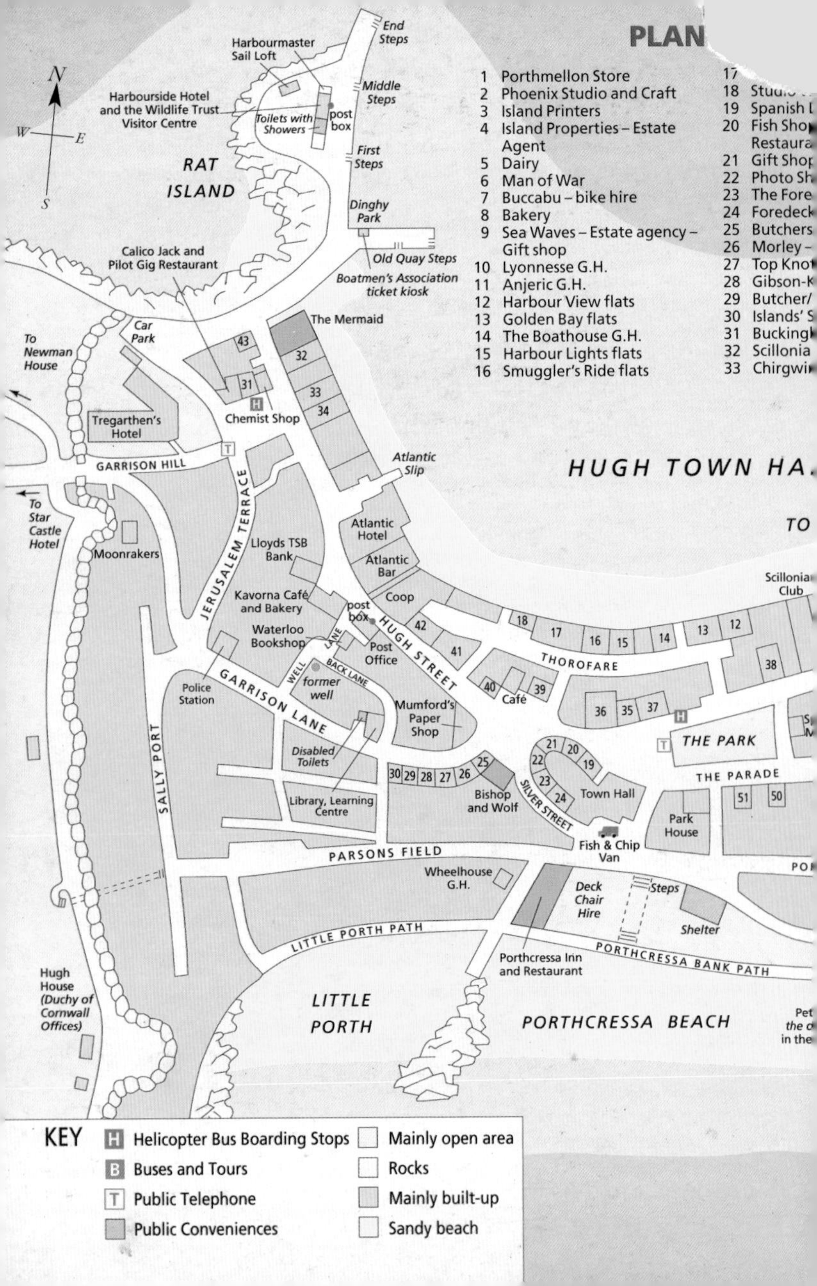

PLAN
1 Porthmellon Store
2 Phoenix Studio and Craft
3 Island Printers
4 Island Properties – Estate Agent
5 Dairy
6 Man of War
7 Buccabu – bike hire
8 Bakery
9 Sea Waves – Estate agency – Gift shop
10 Lyonnesse G.H.
11 Anjeric G.H.
12 Harbour View flats
13 Golden Bay flats
14 The Boathouse G.H.
15 Harbour Lights flats
16 Smuggler's Ride flats
17
18 Studi
19 Spanish
20 Fish Sho
Restaura
21 Gift Shop
22 Photo Sh
23 The Fore
24 Foredeck
25 Butchers
26 Morley –
27 Top Kno
28 Gibson-
29 Butcher/
30 Islands' S
31 Buckingh
32 Scillonia
33 Chirgwi
N
W
E
S
End Steps
Harbourmaster Sail Loft
Middle Steps
Harbourside Hotel and the Wildlife Trust Visitor Centre
Toilets with Showers
post box
First Steps
RAT ISLAND
Dinghy Park
Old Quay Steps
Calico Jack and Pilot Gig Restaurant
Boatmen's Association ticket kiosk
The Mermaid
Car Park
To Newman House
Tregarthen's Hotel
Chemist Shop
GARRISON HILL
HUGH TOWN HA
Atlantic Slip
To Star Castle Hotel
Moonrakers
JERUSALEM TERRACE
Lloyds TSB Bank
Atlantic Hotel
Atlantic Bar
TO
Scillonian Club
Kavorna Café and Bakery
Coop
post box
Waterloo Bookshop
HUGH STREET
Post Office
THOROFARE
WELL LANE
BACK LANE
former well
Police Station
GARRISON LANE
Café
Mumford's Paper Shop
THE PARK
SALLY PORT
Disabled Toilets
Bishop and Wolf
SILVER STREET
Town Hall
THE PARADE
Library, Learning Centre
Park House
Fish & Chip Van
PARSONS FIELD
Wheelhouse G.H.
Deck Chair Hire
Steps
Shelter
LITTLE PORTH PATH
PORTHCRESSA BANK PATH
Porthcressa Inn and Restaurant
Hugh House (Duchy of Cornwall Offices)
LITTLE PORTH
PORTHCRESSA BEACH
KEY
Helicopter Bus Boarding Stops
Buses and Tours
Public Telephone
Public Conveniences
Mainly open area
Rocks
Mainly built-up
Sandy beach

– original drawing by C. Rogers
34 The Sandpiper
35 Chez Michel
36 Bourdeaux Shop
37 Evergreen G.H.
38 Stone Shop
39 Tidelines
40 Shop (Dreaming Sea)
41 Tourist Office and Isles of Scilly Steamship Co.
42 Barclays Bank
43 Pier House
44 Warleggan
45 Trelawney G.H.
46 Marine House G.H.
47 Crebinick G.H.
48 Westford House G.H.
49 Thurleigh G.H.
50 Wingletang G.H.
51 Shearwater G.H.
52 Seaview Moorings G.H.
53 Lemon Hall
54 Shop – All at Sea
55 1st WW seaplane standing
56 Wildlife Trust
PORTH MELLON BEACH
Footpath to Porth Loo and Juliet's Garden
Slip
Lifeboat Station
CARN THOMAS
Windsurfing Centre and Gig House
TELEGRAPH ROAD
INDUSTRIAL ESTATE
Old Junior School
Mincarlo G.H.
Coronation shelter
Millennium Compass Rose
Rechabite Slip
School
Sailing Club
Garage and Island Carriers
Squash Court
Fire Station
Porthmellon Store
Incinerator
Tennis
Dinghy Park
HOLGATES GREEN
THE STRAND
WELL CROSS
St. Mary's Hall Hotel
Methodist Church and Hall
ST MARY'S CHURCH
Garden
Chaplaincy
Catholic Church
post box
CHURCH STREET
CHURCH ROAD
Church Hall
Museum
Methodist Minster's House
Bell Rock Hotel
School boarding house
BRANKSEA CLOSE
BUZZA STREET
Emergency Power Station
footpath
A ROAD
Social Security Office
Launderette
Water tanks
Buzza Tower
footpath up the hill
Hospital and Dentist
Health Centre
footpath to Peninnis
PORTHMELLON INDUSTRIAL ESTATE
Porthmellon Store (retail & wholesale)
St. Mary's Services - Plumbing, Heating, Electrical
Parking Area
Garden & Décor
Richard Hand General Haulage Contractor
Sibley's Fuel & Marine Fuel Merchants
Phoenix Stained Glass Studio & Craft Centre
I.S.S. Co. Ltd. Marine & General Engineering
A.H. Read & Son Printers, Office & PC Supplies
Jim Heslin - Isles of Scilly Underwater Centre
Roy Tatler - Qualified Motor Engineer
Squash Court
Emergency Services - Unmanned Emergency Tel.No.999
M.J. Nightingale - General Builder & Concrete Products
Alec Hicks - House & Sons Joinery Workshop
Island Properties Estate Agents & Holiday Lets
Scillonia Building Supplies for Wood, Cement Etc.
David Parr Engineering
Pernic Forge - Welding & General Engineering
Quadron Services Ltd.
Rat Island Sailboat Company
Sibley's Fuel & Marine Fuel Merchants
Nike Engineering (Marine Engineers)
Isles of Scilly Bakery
Chiverton Builders

BIRDS

Although a wide range of passage migrants use Scilly as a halting place in spring and autumn, Scilly has only about sixty breeding species (Cornwall has over twice this number), and about fifteen of these are seabirds. The Herring Gull is not as numerous in Scilly as formerly – indeed, there are probably more wrens in Scilly; but its laughing cry is ubiquitous – the ha ha ha so familiar to Scilly's human residents that they are scarcely aware of it – and betokens no amusement on the part of the bird; like its equally distinctive raucous call, it is an expression of excitement or of apprehension, the degree of rapidity indicating the amount of alarm.

In addition, there have been some very rare sightings of about 200 other species including White Stork, Purple Heron, Little Bittern and even, in 1999, of a North American Night Hawk and a Short-toed Eagle (*Ciraetus gallicus*). Many are vagrants from other continents blown off course by winds. Apart from these, Scilly usually has no Owls, Woodpeckers, Nuthatches, Magpies or Buntings.

To see waterfowl, birdwatchers are recommended to go to Great and Little Pools (Bryher), Tresco Great Pool, Porth Hellick Pool, and Big and Little Pools (St. Agnes); but the best spots for viewing seabirds are Men-a-vaur, Hanjague, Castle Bryher, Mincarlo, Teän, St. Helen's, Gorregan, Menawethan, and Annet, and rocks in their proximity. But access to most of these islands is restricted – the greatest danger to birds, after natural disasters and oil slicks, being disturbance by humans. Seabirds have declined in numbers in Scilly in recent years, some breeding species by as much as forty per cent. Reasons suggested for this decline include human disturbance, intensive fishing in the surrounding waters of Britain which may have reduced food supplies, and pollution, as evidenced from the increasing debris from passing ships coming ashore in Scilly. There is also pollution from oil slicks far out at sea which, although dissipated long before any trace of them can reach Scilly, often disable birds alighting on the sea to feed or rest during their long ocean flights. Shags, Great Black-backed Gulls and Common Terns show a particular decline in numbers, while Fulmars increase, as they do in other parts of Britain.

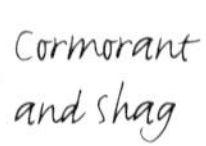

Cormorant and shag

Of the seabirds of Scilly, only the Cormorants, Herring Gulls and Great Black-backed Gulls reside all the year; Lesser Black-backed Gulls, Guillemots, Razorbills, Puffins, Manx Shearwaters, Fulmars, Kittiwakes and Storm Petrels arrive in spring, many of them having spent the winter at sea. Terns arrive from West Africa towards the end of April. All these birds come to Scilly to make nests and breed, so boat trips to see them start in April.

The seabirds fall into five main groups: cormorants; gannets; gulls and terns; auks; and petrels and shearwaters. Of the first group the green-eyed **Shag** is seen in Scilly in large numbers, often in great rafts on the sea. But it nests singly, and will defend its young staunchly with much bluster and hissing. It has black plumage and sports a short crest in the breeding season. The **Common Cormorant**, by contrast, has no crest but a white chin; it breeds in large colonies, its nests filthy and smelly from the rotting remains of fish on which its young have fed. One can often watch a Common Cormorant diving for fish and observe that it may sometimes be submerged for up to a minute. Though the Common Cormorant is three feet long (six inches taller than the Shag), it is a more timid bird, even deserting its young if it feels itself in danger. Both birds have the curious habit of standing motionless on a rock with wings fully outstretched; one explanation of this is that the birds have insufficient waterproofing oil for their feathers and are drying out, but others believe that the bird's strange poise is an assertion of territorial possession or perhaps a recognition that there is food in the vicinity and that they are claiming fishing rights. Another suggestion – from research carried out at Neumünster Zoo – is that the birds are defrosting their injested food – exposing their bellies to the sunlight to speed up their digestion of cold fish. Drying-out is still the favoured explanation, but much of mystery attaches to birds; for instance, mammals in their early stages of development are female until, in the course of growth, some become male; but with birds the process is the other way round.

Gannets

The **Gannet** (or Solan Goose) has a six-foot wing span and is the largest British seabird. It is white with black wing tips, and may be seen cruising by or making spectacular dives after fish from a considerable height. Gannets are faithful to one mate all their lives, which may be about twenty years. They do not breed in Scilly, although over half the world's Gannets breed around the British Isles.

The most formidable of seabirds in Scilly is the **Great Black-backed Gull** which has a wing span of over five feet and is as big as a goose. It is a killer of Puffins and Manx Shearwaters and will even prey on rats and rabbits. It is white with black upper parts, and has a savage-looking, yellow and red bill.

Great Black-backed Gulls

Lesser Black-backed Gulls

It is liable to dive upon anyone unwise enough to intrude into its nesting colonies. Smaller, but similar, is the **Lesser Black-backed Gull**, which has slatey-grey upper parts and yellow rather than pink legs.

The **Herring Gull** has much lighter-coloured upper parts than the Lesser Black-backed Gull and is remarkably tame locally and a useful scavenger of beaches. The young of all three gulls keep some of their immature brown feathers for up to four years after leaving the nest, and so are easily distinguished from adult birds.

Herring Gulls

In the summer they are often to be seen worrying the life out of their parents for some regurgitated food.

Black-headed gulls

Another gull is the **Kittiwake**, which gets its name from its pleasant-sounding call, '*Kittiwaak*'. It is a small oceanic gull with blue-grey upper parts, dark eyes and distinctive black legs. It nests in colonies on precarious ledges using the same nest each year if it can, its droppings performing the useful function of cementing the nest material together. If the young take one step from their nests, they will tumble into the sea, so they remain immobile from the day they hatch to the day they fly – just sitting still, growing.

Kittiwakes

Sandwich, Common and Roseate Terns

Smaller relatives of the gulls are the slender Sea Swallows with long forked tails, the **Common, Arctic, Sandwich and Roseate Terns**, whose nests are mere scrapes in the sand. The considerable aerobatic skills of the **Common Tern** make it one of the most interesting birds to watch, and it will often be seen in Scilly busily diving for fish in shallow waters; but, whereas the Gannet neatly folds its wings an instant before it enters the sea from its dive, the Common Tern continues to flap all the way into the water with much splash. The arch-migrator is the **Arctic Tern**, many of whom each year travel from the Antarctic to the Arctic and back again – an amazing feat.

The commonest of the auks is the **Razorbill**, which is black above and white below, with a large bill crossed by a white line. Like other auks it has short, stubby wings and has to beat them rapidly to stay aloft. It lays a single egg and sits on it in an upright, standing posture looking a bit uncomfortable. In Scilly, about two in every hundred of the browner, dagger-billed **Guillemots** have unusual markings consisting of a white line around the eye continuing backwards on each side of the head – looking a little as if they are wearing white spectacles. These are the **Bridled Guillemots**. The Guillemot's egg is remarkably elongated so that it will roll only in a circle, which prevents it falling off the narrow ledge or crevice on which it is laid.

Razorbill and Guillemot

A third auk is the little, plump **Puffin** or Sea-Parrot, which breeds in burrows (sometimes using old rabbit holes) on Annet and a few smaller islands. Puffins were much valued for their meat in the Middle Ages – 300 of them being paid to the Black Prince as part of the rent by the tenant-owner of Scilly in 1337. At that time they were even classed as fish so that they could be eaten in Lent.

To the human eye the Puffin is a sweet bird, if rather a clown to watch. Its take-off involves vigorous, propulsive beating of the sea with its wings, causing cascades of spray in all directions in its efforts to achieve enough lift to become airborne – although once aloft it is a fine flier. Landing seems equally comical, as it is lacking in the self-assurance normally associated with the flight of many seabirds. The Puffin contrives to escape from enemies such as the Great Black-backed Gull by diving below the surface, where it beats its wings to propel itself along underwater – unlike the Cormorant, for example, which does a doggy-paddle. The Puffin's most outstanding feature, which is discarded after the breeding season, is its multicoloured, parrot-like sheath on its bill, which looks quite artificial set on its white face with red-rimmed eyes. This attractive feature is an ornament to attract a mate, but also a weapon with which to fight for territory and a shovel to dig out its burrow. The Puffin only comes to land to breed, laying a single egg, and, by the end of July, nearly all the Puffins will have left Scilly to spend the rest of the year far out at sea. Auks have been called the Penguins of the Atlantic; they cannot glide or soar, so perhaps – in evolutionary terms – they, too, are on the way to flightlessness.

Puffin

The petrels and shearwaters, relatives of the Albatross, also only come to land to breed; in fact, the mysterious **Manx Shearwater** has one of its very few English breeding colonies on Annet. Rafts of Manx Shearwaters can be seen floating on the sea awaiting dusk because terror of the Greater Black-backed Gull induces them to enter and leave their nests only under cover of darkness, at which time their strange crowing calls can be heard. The name Shearwater comes from the bird's unmistakeable flight; it skims the surface of the sea, canting first to one side and then to the other so that its black upper and white lower parts show alternately. The larger, whitish **Fulmar Petrel** (Northern Fulmar) nests on cliff ledges on rocks such as Men-a-vaur, and has a surprising defence weapon; if threatened, it will squirt any intruder, including man, with an unpleasant smelling, oily liquid. The **Storm Petrel** or Mother Carey's Chicken also nests in Scilly but is rarely seen because it is nocturnal. It feeds on plankton and is the smallest of all European seabirds, returning each year to Annet to nest under the boulders.

Fulmars

Many visitors are intrigued by the numerous small birds in Scilly which wade in the shallow waters along the sea-shore. Among these are **Sanderlings**: they are small, pale grey-and-white birds, usually seen in groups, and they have the habit of running in and out of the sea as the waves lap the sandy shore. They seem to dare each other to get their feet wet but, just at the last moment, think better of it. They fly off together and then, after a short flight, return almost to where they were before. They have been described as looking like mechanical toys. Many of them have come from Greenland and appear tame when they first land on the beaches of Scilly, for they may not have seen humans before. In addition there are the following:

Sanderling

Turnstones

Turnstones. These are about the size of a thrush, plump and chesty. They frequent pebbly beaches in groups and turn over pieces of seaweed and small stones searching for sandhoppers and insects.

Ringed Plovers. They have bold markings, and black and white heads with black collars. They are broad in front and narrow behind, and have a hurried walk. Their numbers are in decline.

Ringed Plover

Oystercatchers. These handsome, black-and-white birds have pink legs and utter loud, piping cries. The Oystercatcher's most distinctive feature is a bright orange bill more than three inches long. Most of the tidal rocks of Scilly are covered with limpets which are not hard to dislodge at the first blow, but subsequent attacks only serve to tighten their hold, and, indeed, the shell of the limpet will break before its grip is loosened. But the Oystercatcher has developed a technique for dealing with such shellfish, and its long bill is also ideal for pricking and probing for eggs, worms, and similar morsels. Cockleshells abound in Scilly, and small piles of recently discarded and broken ones may well indicate where an Oystercatcher has had a meal. The Oystercatcher and the Ringed Plover are the only two species of wader to breed in the islands.

Oystercatchers

Two attractive land birds are the shore-loving **Rock Pipit**, a greyish brown bird which has a remarkable parachuting song-flight, and the gorse-loving **Stonechat**, the male of which is a handsome, plump bird with a black head, an orange breast, and long white panels on its brown wings. Blackbirds, Starlings and House Sparrows are remarkable for having adapted to taking the abundant nectar from plants in Scilly, especially in Tresco Abbey Garden, where some of them seem unusually tame.

Cuckoos arrive in Scilly from Africa in early April, usually before they are heard on the mainland. The call of the male cuckoo – the female is silent – is heard widely in Scilly in April, while the female is locating the nests of up to five or six species of small birds, but all insect-eaters not seed-eaters. Cuckoos lay about four different types of eggs, varying in their markings to provide a closer match to the host's eggs; this may only be evolved behaviour, but strikes humans as devilishly clever.

Artist: Sue Dibley
(Not drawn to the same scale)

BIRD SPOTTER'S CHECK LIST

A – Residents	Where spotted in Scilly
Blackbird	
Blue Tit	
Canada Goose	
Carrion Crow	
Chaffinch	
Collared Dove	
Common Cormorant	
Coot	
Dunnock	
Gadwall	
Goldcrest (Europe's smallest bird)	
Great Black-backed Gull	
Great Tit	
Greenfinch	
Herring Gull	
House Sparrow (more colourful in Scilly than his urban counterpart)	
Kestrel	
Mallard	
Moorhen	
Mute Swan	
Oystercatcher	
Peregrine (resident since 1975 and breeding)	
Pheasant	
Raven (breeding in Eastern Isles since 1981)	
Ringed Plover	
Robin	
Rock Pipit	
Shag	
Skylark	
Song Thrush (numerous)	
Starling	
Stock Dove	
Stonechat	
Teal	
Tufted Duck	
Wood Pigeon	
Wren	
B – Summer Visitors	
Blackcap (some over winter)	
Chiffchaff (some over winter)	
Common Tern	
Cuckoo	
Fulmar (bred in Scilly since 1951)	
Goldfinch	

	Where spotted in Scilly
Guillemot	
House Martin	
Jackdaw	
Kittiwake	
Lesser Black-backed Gull	
Linnet	
Manx Shearwater	
Puffin	
Razorbill	
Reed Warbler	
Sandwich Tern	
Sedge Warbler	
Shelduck (bred for first time in Scilly 1958)	
Storm Petrel	
Swallow	
Turtle Dove	
Wheatear	
Willow Warbler	
C – Migrants & Winter Visitors	
Arctic Tern	
Bar-tailed Godwit	
Black-headed Gull	
Bridled Tern (July 1991)	
Bullfinch	
Coal Tit	
Common Gull	
Common Sandpiper	
Curlew	
Dotterel	
Dunlin	
Gannet (seen in Scilly over the sea all year)	
Goldeneye	
Golden Oriole	
Great Northern Diver	
Lapwing	
Meadow Pipit	
Mistle Thrush (a few)	
Pied Wagtail	
Redshank	
Redwing	
Sanderling (many to be seen on the beaches)	
Sand Martin	
Snipe (common in Scilly in winter)	
Swift	
Turnstone (many seen in Scilly all the year)	
Roseate Tern	

THE SEA IN SCILLY

'There is all summer in the sound of the sea' – Walt Whitman.

Photo: Keith Dibley.

'But what is there to do in Scilly?' 'For a start, how about looking at the sea?'

What is this life if, full of care,
We have no time to stand and stare? – W. H. Davies

In sunlight the seawater around the Scillies is one of the great attractions of the islands, pure, fresh and colourful. In its agelong conflict with the granite rocks, its swell breaks cleanly, carpeting the ocean surface with white, salty foam; yet, in calmer, greener patches – as in the photograph above – the water is translucent to a depth, with only, above water, the head of an inquiring Grey Seal checking who's calling.

Visitors find the Scilly Islands small and the surrounding sea large – for someone is sure to have mentioned the 3,000 miles of open ocean westward to America. An especial pleasure in Scilly is to join one of the numerous boat trips that take place each summer morning from St. Mary's quay. The longest is to the Bishop Rock seven miles out, and is usually an exciting adventure – a novel one for many who live in inland areas – and a sure way of blowing away accumulated mainland cobwebs.

The interest in the trip is not only in visiting an isolated pillar lighthouse or even in sightseeing for seabirds and seals, but it can also be an exhilarating experience in a running sea. On the outward voyage the launch climbs its way up Atlantic rollers, while, on the return journey, it is lifted forward before dropping back into the trough astern as each roller overtakes. The movement is mostly too quick to occasion queasiness, and can be likened more to the fun of the fair but without the artificiality.

How different the beach at near low water springs, an ebbing tide emptying the bay, leaving a motionless expanse of sand, rounded pebbles and small abandoned puddles. Then, in a quiet moment, hard to discern but controlled by awesome, unseen forces of the moon and the sun, the tide it turns and the water reverses, oozing back over land it so recently vacated. Like spring among the seasons, the water's flow is predictable and regular, but 700 times more frequent; that in Scilly is big enough to wipe away the footprints and sandcastles of many morning incursions, in refreshing, twice-a-day cleansings – with larger spring-cleans around the new and full moons – leaving, after each, the same level, unspoilt, pristine playground that was there before.

Towards high water, the waves recoil, often in powerful bursts against the rocks, or they advance in long, progressive lines across the margins of the sandy beach, lifting, rolling, breaking, and subsiding, each a distinctive force, no two exactly the same. Some waves challenge the backwash of a spent predecessor, others seem content to ride its back, breaking feebly in hurried flurry – a sight of soothing therapy, harmonising attention with one of nature's lasting rhythms in a mesmerising diversion from passing human concerns. Discover, too, an optical illusion: the waves rush in but, save for motion up and down promoted by displaced energy from far-distant storms, the water hardly shifts position at all; and another wonderful thing about this theatre – there is no entrance fee. Swinburne wrote:

Time has no power in this tranquil place,
Here nothing stirs save whence the restless tide
Retreats, returns, changes its fickle mind,
And bares again the rocks it strove to hide.

VISITORS' QUESTIONNAIRES

Some visitors to Scilly filled in questionnaires about their likes and dislikes concerning their holidays in the Islands.

LIKES included their appreciation of the beauty of the Scillies, the friendliness of the inhabitants, the feeling of safety, holidaying without the car, the relatively slower pace of life, the large number of varied and interesting boat trips, the lack of traffic (outside of Hugh Town), the wonderful wildlife, beaches and walks, and the good accommodation, together with praise for the three travel operators, British International, *Scillonian III* and Skybus. One visitor liked the democratic spirit in Scilly, where the rich do not flaunt their wealth and where there are no obvious signs of poverty or yobbery.

DISLIKES included some of the travel costs, the traffic in Hugh Town, the lack of a heated sea, and going home. Nearly a third of visitors came from the Home Counties and a quarter from the West Country.

About 80% of visitors stayed on St. Mary's, 9% on Tresco, 5% on St. Martin's, 4% on Bryher and 2% on St. Agnes – this last island being the only inhabited off-island without a hotel. Just over a third of visitors stayed in self-catering, another third in guest houses, a quarter in hotels and the rest on camping sites or with friends.

SHARKS, PORPOISES, DOLPHINS, SEALS

The harmless **Basking Shark** is sometimes seen around the Isles of Scilly. It is one of the giant fish and may be over thirty feet in length. Its dorsal fin, clearly visible above the surface, seems menacing as the shark glides ponderously through the water. In fact, bathers have nothing to fear; a Basking Shark is not interested in anything larger than a shrimp. It spends its life sifting the water for small crustaceans and other plankton, which it strains with its gill clefts and rakers. Launches often go to within a few yards of them. They were hunted off Norway and Ireland, mainly for the forty gallons of oil which the average shark carries in its liver, a low grade oil used primarily in tanning. Though the flesh of this shark is edible, it is not very palatable, and one has to be rather hungry to enjoy eating it.

Porpoises are seen around the islands in files of half-a-dozen or more and take little notice of boats. The Porpoise rises out of the water in a graceful curve as it moves along, and the intake of its breath is very audible. In former days a file of Porpoises may well have been mistaken for a sea-serpent. **Common Dolphins** are also occasionally seen in the sea around Scilly in large schools. They are larger than Porpoises, and have the habit of leaping out of the water. A recent claim is that dolphins (in this case Bottlenose) have been shown to recognise themselves in a mirror.

Colonies of inquisitive and friendly **Grey Seals** are to be found on the outlying rocks of Scilly. At low water they can often be observed out of the sea apparently sunning themselves on rocks where they have been left by the receding tide. When approached too closely, they lollop cumbrously down the rocks to the water's edge and slide into the sea, where their heads, resembling those of large dogs, keep bobbing up above the surface as they watch the intruding boat.

The Grey Seal is the largest animal to breed wild in the British Isles and grows to a length of eight feet; it is found only in the Atlantic and the seas of Northern Europe. The seal pup is under three feet long when born in early autumn, and looks most attractive clad in creamy white fur, which it loses after four weeks. By the end of its first three weeks of life, it is deserted by its mother, who will no longer suckle it, and it is left to fend for itself. This helps to explain the high mortality rate of the young, which may be as much as sixty per cent. Seals have the richest milk known – fifty per cent is fat. Those which survive infancy may live for twenty or thirty years. Scars are sometimes seen on the necks of bulls which testify to some ferocious fighting between them. 40% of the world's grey seals are around Britain's western coasts.

OTHER FAUNA

The **Scilly Shrew** is unique to Scilly. It is a sub-species of the Lesser White-toothed Shrew which is found nowhere else in the United Kingdom. It has a large appetite and consumes almost its own body weight every day. Shrews are inquisitive creatures, but shy and not often seen alive (see P.67). Sometimes they are seen 'caravanning', when the mother shrew leads up to six young ones in line, each holding on to the one in front, nose to tail. In Scilly there are no foxes, badgers, moles, stoats, weasels, squirrels, hares, voles, snakes, toads, newts or horseflies, and not a great number of wasps. It is claimed that the absence of these, together with environmental factors of geography and climate, are responsible for detectable variations in the evolution and behaviour of some of the fauna in Scilly. There used to be no **Hedgehogs** in Scilly but,

BUTTERFLIES OF SCILLY

Artist: Sue Dibley

Meadow Brown – 55mm female
Scilly's most common butterfly is the Meadow Brown. On the underside of its hind wings there are a variable number of spots (false eyes) from none at all to five. On St. Mary's, St. Martin's and Tresco, there is a very similar spot distribution, whereas the spot patterns of Meadow Browns on the smaller islands show considerable differences, and on Teän vary even between the northern and southern parts of the island – as many as three distinguishable communities have been found on the island.

Common Blue – 35mm male
The Common Blue is bright blue on the uppersides of its wings, with interrupted orange bands and black spots underneath. The female has more brown upper sides. On Scilly the blue is more extensive and almost silvery. The spots on the underside of the wings tend to run together. In Scilly it commonly lays its egg on *Bird's-foot Trefoil*.

Small Tortoiseshell – 50mm male
A striking butterfly with orange-and-black wings bordered with half moons. It enjoys the sun and is often found flocking around Buddleias, Thistles and Nettles.

Butterflies seem flimsy fliers but some are capable of long flights. Varieties such as ***Painted Lady*** and ***Red Admiral*** cross the English Channel to Scilly from about June in good summers. In September they set off on the return journey to North Africa.

Artist: Sue Dibley

SHELLS

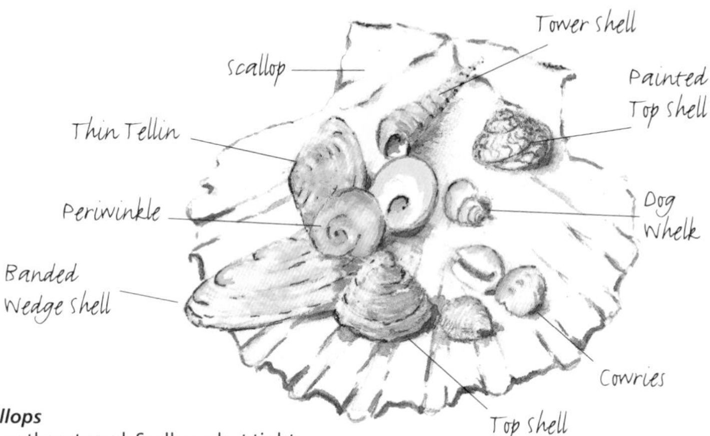

Scallops

When threatened, Scallops shut tight and shoot backwards – they can survive for about fifteen years.

Thin Tellin

Thin Tellins lie just under the sand.

Cowries

There are two types of cowries to be found in Scilly. The European Cowrie has three dark spots on top of its pink shell, while the Arctic Cowrie has none. They are delicate and finely marked shells, prized as counters. In Scilly they used to be known as moneypennies.

Periwinkles

Small, colourful shells in yellow, orange, red, brown or green, Popular with beachcombing collectors.

Top Shell

These shells are conical in shape on a broad base, and often with pink or purple streaks. They are particularly attractive when, as the shell becomes worn, mother-of-pearl shows through.

Razor Shells

These abound in Scilly on beaches at low water. They are so called owing to their similarity to cut-throat razors.

Limpets

Limpets cling tightly to rocks except when the tide covers them and they then move about feeding. But they always return to the same spot on their rock. Most limpets start life as males and later become females.

Limpet
Dog Whelk
Blue-rayed Limpet
Razor Shell

in about 1981, they appeared on St. Mary's (as on Lundy someone introduced them) and have increased in numbers. It is said that three were brought over from the mainland as a birthday present for a Scillonian girl but, as they are notoriously difficult to keep in captivity, all escaped. One was found dead the next day, and a second was run over a week later, but not before he had made the third one pregnant, and it is from her that the present population is believed to be descended. Slow Worms were introduced to Bryher in the 1950s in a similar casual fashion, and for that reason it is no longer accurate to claim that Scilly has no lizards.

On Samson, and on some of the smaller islands, there are black rabbits, while on St. Helen's there are both black and white ones. One of the most popular picture postcards in local shops used to be of two donkeys under the caption 'Two Scilly Asses', but few donkeys are kept in Scilly nowadays. There used to be many, and before motor transport they were used to pull the cartloads of wooden boxes of early Scillonian flowers to the quay for export to the mainland. Between the wars they were also harnessed to jingles, which could be hired by visitors to take themselves around St. Mary's, but the animals tended to be obstinate and selective of the routes they would go, some visitors finding themselves taken involuntarily in the jingle to the end of the quay, as if they were for export.

THE SHIPWRECK OF SIR CLOUDESLEY SHOVELL

The rocks of the Isles of Scilly have earned an evil reputation among seamen for the danger to shipping that they represent.

Rear-Admiral Sir Cloudesley Shovell, the 57-year-old commander-in-chief, and a national hero of his day, was returning home from the Mediterranean to Portsmouth with gold and silver coins, bronze cannon and the like. On 22nd October, 1707, unsure of his position, he ordered the fleet to heave-to to take soundings. From the information available his navigators miscalculated the fleet's position, an error in navigation which was the cause of the disaster which followed. Believing the English Channel clear before him, Sir Cloudesley ordered his ships forward – to destruction on the rocks of Scilly. It resulted in one of the worst disasters in Britain's peacetime naval history, when four large ships of a fleet of twenty-one were wrecked on the Western Rocks with the loss of about 1,670 men.

It seems remarkable that men of so much experience should have been so far out in reckoning their position, but may be partly explained by failure to allow sufficiently for the inaccuracy of charts; and perhaps, on that blustery night, the fire was burning low in the cresset at the top of St. Agnes lighthouse. As a consequence of the disaster, the government offered money to somebody who could determine longitude. Harrison won this prize by inventing a timepiece which would keep time accurately on a moving vessel at sea. But Shovell's navigational error would appear to have been a miscalculation more of latitude than of longitude.

Four ships struck on the Western Rocks and foundered. The flagship, the 90-gun *Association*, a second rate, 1,459 ton ship-of-the-line, together with the 70-gun *Eagle*, were lost with all hands. The *Eagle* is thought to have sunk on Tearing Ledge south-east of Bishop Rock. The 48-gun *Romney* fared little better for only her quartermaster, George Lawrence, was saved. The crew of the fourth vessel, the 8-gun fireship *Firebrand*, were more fortunate as twenty-five survived the wreck. Sir George Byng, in the *Royal Anne* of 100 guns, was to windward of the *Association*. He heard the breakers but only saved his ship by setting her topsails when within a ship's length of disaster, and not before his quarter-boat had been carried away by passing too close to a rock called Trenemene.

When the *Association* struck, a signal gun was fired, warning following ships to alter course. According to some accounts, Shovell took to his barge, together with his treasure chest and pet greyhound; but, in the sea conditions, this is now regarded as unlikely, as is the tale that Shovell came ashore and was murdered by a Scillonian woman for the sake of a ring on his finger. There is also no evidence for the oft-repeated story that among the crew of the *Association* was a Scillonian who was punished for trying to warn Shovell that the ships were heading for the rocks. In fact, Shovell's body was found floating in the sea, and was at first buried in a shallow grave above the shoreline of Porth Hellick at a spot now marked by a rough granite monument. Later, it was disinterred and taken to London, where, after a State funeral, it was laid to rest in Westminster Abbey. Over his tomb in the Abbey, is an ornate if not very beautiful memorial by Grinling Gibbons. More pleasing is the magnificent Royal Coat of Arms of Queen Anne in the Council Chambers (No. 1 Court) in the Civic Buildings, Penzance, which is actually from the sternboard of the *Association*. It was presented to the citizens of Penzance by the inhabitants of Scilly in appreciation of help given to the islanders in one of their periods of starvation.

Evidence which seems to support the theory that Shovell did manage to take to his barge is that, whereas most of the bodies of the hapless crew of the *Association*, none of whom survived, were taken up from the shore or the sea around St. Agnes, Shovell's body was found at Porth Hellick on St. Mary's, together with that of Captain Loades and, nearby, the bodies of Shovell's two Narborough stepsons – all people likely to have been taken in the Admiral's barge if it had been successfully launched. Even the body of Shovell's pet greyhound – his name still on his collar – was found at Porth Hellick, yet another pointer to Shovell having sailed his barge the 6 nautical miles from the Western Rocks to St. Mary's, and possibly suggesting that Shovell was wrecked a second time that night on the only other rock named Gilstone in the Scillies, which just happens to be located near the entrance to the bay at Porth Hellick. Of some support to this seemingly far-fetched scenario is that, apart from a graze over one eye, Shovell's rotund figure, when located, showed no signs of prolonged battering at sea or against rocks, which might have been expected if it had journeyed in the water that distance from the wreck. This matter is interestingly discussed – if not resolved – in the fascinating book *Sir Cloudesley Shovell* by Simon Harris, who makes the valid point that, although Shovell is mostly forgotten today, in his day he was almost as famous as Nelson became nearly a century later. Pepys disliked him, but this may have had something to do with Shovell coming, like Nelson, from a Norfolk family of modest origins.

The Admiral's flagship, the *Association*, had gone down in about ninety feet of water, but it was not until 1967 that divers discovered, in the area where she had sunk, what was to prove one of the most valuable underwater treasure sites around the British Isles. Hoards of 17th-century gold and silver coins, including many Spanish pieces-of-eight, were discovered wedged in rock crevices or lying scattered on the sea-bed under the rocks, together with several bronze cannon and many other ship's objects. Eventually, a silver plate bearing Shovell's crest was brought to the surface by divers, and this positively identified the wreck site as that of the *Association*. Much treasure probably still remains to be lifted from Shovell's stricken ships, but diving in such waters can be hazardous. Wreck sites in Scilly are hard to locate because all but a few traces of the ships have disappeared, their hulls pulled apart by the tremendous power of the surging sea and then covered by shifting sand.

OTHER WRECKS

There are about 900 recorded shipwrecks around the Scillies over the centuries; one of these, the 74-gun *Colossus*, one of Nelson's ships, was returning to England in 1798 in a leaky condition, when she foundered near Southward Wells off Samson. Several cases of vases, part of the priceless collection of classical art treasures belonging to Sir William Hamilton, were lost in the seaweed and their location not discovered until 1975. They can now be seen in the British Museum. Another disaster was that of the German transatlantic liner *Schiller*, bound from New York, which struck on the Retarrier Ledges in fog on 7th May 1875. Of the 355 people on board, the survivors were only forty-four men and one woman – but none of the children – only two of the eight lifeboats getting away safely. Many bodies were later buried in Old Town churchyard.

On 14th December, 1907, the unique, American-owned *Thomas W. Lawson* was wrecked in Scilly, the only vessel ever constructed with seven masts. She was over 5,000 tons and bound from Philadelphia to London carrying 2¼ million gallons of lubricating oil. At daybreak the ship was seen bottom up on the Outer Ranneys rocks near Annet. For some time afterwards St. Agnes was surrounded on its shore-line with an odious film of oil, possibly the world's first oil spillage disaster.

The largest ship to be wrecked near Scilly was the 61,000 ton tanker *Torrey Canyon* in 1967 on the Seven Stones reef, eight miles north-east of St. Martin's. The oil spillage drifted away from Scilly, but caused more than £3 million worth of damage on the coast of Cornwall before the tanker was eventually destroyed by aerial bombing. Seabirds suffered greatly and numbers declined, particularly of Guillemots which are very susceptible to oil and have only one chick a year.

One of the most valuable wreck sites was discovered after intensive search in 1971. This was the Dutch East Indiaman *Hollandia* which sank north-west of Annet on 13th July 1743, on her maiden voyage from the Texel with a huge cargo of silver. This was followed in 1973 by the discovery of the wreck site of the *Princess Maria* which went down in 1686.

In 1974 a wreck was found which was presumed to be that of the 1,050 ton Dutch East Indiaman *Zeelilie* (Sea Lily), which sailed from the East bound for the Netherlands in 1795 carrying tea, spices, porcelain and perhaps some gold, but *en route* was captured by the British. Of the prize-crew on board, twenty-five were drowned when she struck the Western Rocks, and little of the ship has yet been found on the wreck-site except cannon, shards, a pillar dollar coin and an ancient Chinese porcelain demigod of the Ming Dynasty.

Many old wrecks still elude detection and, despite sophisticated navigational equipment, marine accidents continue to occur. In March, 1997, the 3,083 ton *Cita*, owned by thirteen Hamburg dentists and bound for Ireland, was sixteen miles off course and ran into Newfoundland Point off Porth Hellick when her senior crew were asleep. No lives were lost, but the vessel became a total loss and later sank, her mixed cargo bursting out of many of her 200 containers, with all manner of goods coming ashore including shirts, golf bags, trainers, doors, batteries, kitchen scales and motor tyres. The most lasting legacies were shivers of polythene, torn from bags originally bound for Irish shops – which, although fortunately transparent, still somewhat disfigure the upper reaches of some of Scilly's beaches such as Old Town – and the estimated 2,400 miles of polyester film (of the type used in video tapes) which came ashore, but which was mostly collected and found a use as fibre-filling in duvets and garments.

In the same year on 16th May, on leaving Scilly, the German-owned, 24,800 ton cruise ship *Albatross*, formerly the Cunard liner *Sylvania*, ran on to the Bartholomew Ledges between St. Mary's and the Gugh, tearing a hole in her starboard hull large enough for a diver to enter. The ship developed a list but her double-hull saved her from sinking, her 500 passengers being taken safely to Penzance in *Scillonian III*.

LIGHTHOUSES AND LIFEBOATS

The earliest lighthouse in Scilly was completed in 1680 on St. Agnes. It is painted white to serve also as a daymark. Its use was discontinued when the automatic Peninnis light was built in 1911. The most famous is the **Bishop Rock Lighthouse** situated just under six miles from St. Mary's, a lone sentinel standing on the most distant and outermost rock in the archipelago, and a graceful and stately pillar of fine proportions. Originally it was of cast-iron with open legs in the belief that rough seas would pass through them without harm – but a gale in 1850 swept all of it away. A granite tower, 120 feet high, was then erected, but the spray went right over it; so, in 1887, the whole structure was encased and given two extra storeys, bringing it to 175 feet above mean sea level – the highest of pillar lights. In gales, the lamp at its top, 175 feet above the sea, is calculated to swing through an arc of up to six feet.

There used to be about 300 lighthouse keepers around Britain's coast; but now just two operators per shift, sitting in their control room at Harwich in Essex, control all seventy-two lighthouses. Indeed, satellite navigation and global positioning systems, assisted by shore-based reference sites, are now so accurate, that shipping has little real need of lights in the 21st century, except in emergencies and for re-insurance; and, as is the case already with nearly 400 Trinity House buoys, they may all become solar-powered in time.

Round Island Lighthouse, to the north of the islands, stands 132 feet above mean sea level on a circular-shaped island; its white light flashes once every ten seconds. Beyond the Isles of Scilly, to the north-east, lie the rocks named the **Seven Stones**, where an engineless lightship is moored. She has been known to break away from her moorings and drift – it last happened in 1999. To the east lie the **Wolf, Pendeen, Tater-du,** the **Longships** off Land's End, and **The Lizard**.

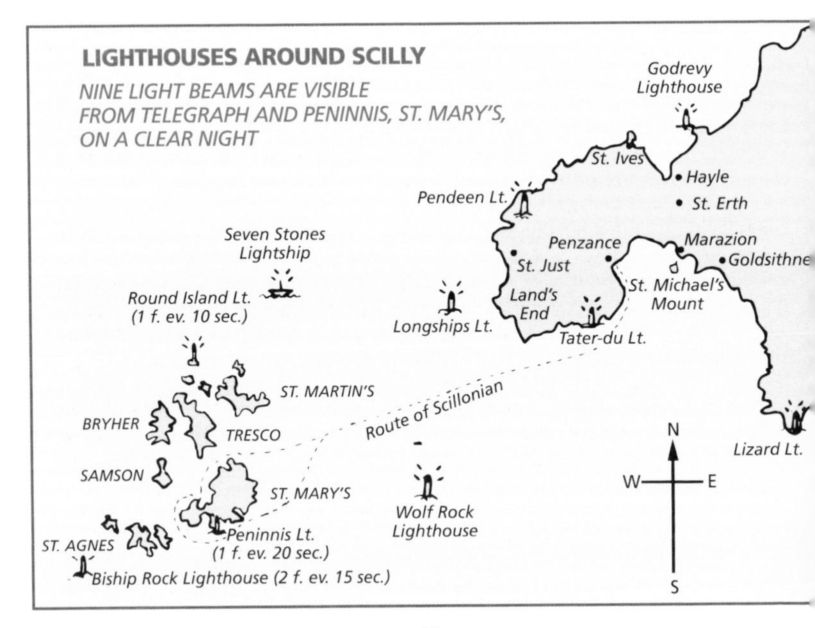

The lifeboat stationed at St. Mary's since 1998 is the 17-metre, 25-knot Severn class *The Whiteheads*, seven knots faster than her predecessor the Arun class *Robert Edgar*. The crew, who are volunteers, hold themselves in readiness to answer calls for help. They are normally summoned by telephone or personal pager, but, before launching the tender, two maroons are often fired making a loud enough noise to be heard in most parts of St. Mary's. Over 650 lives have been saved by the crews of Scilly's lifeboats since 1874. The lifeboat house is open to view by the public in the summer, and the tender can be seen. *The Whiteheads* is too big to be housed in the lifeboat house, but can usually be seen riding at anchor in the harbour at St. Mary's, in a condition of readiness so that she can put to sea quickly at any time to help a vessel in distress.

HISTORY AND ANTIQUITIES

In old records Scilly appears variously as Sulla (similar to the name of a pre-Roman water goddess), Sullye, Sulli, Sulley, and Sully (sun islands). The intrusive 'c' did not appear in the name until the 16th century. The English word '*silly*' has a common origin with the German word '*selig*' meaning 'blessed' or 'holy', and this may provide an explanation for Scilly's name.

The islands of Scilly are the surviving hill-tops of a much larger land area, the extent of which we can only surmise from the fact that, at the fifteen metre mark, most of the present islands become part of one large one. The drowning of the valleys of this densely-wooded island most likely came about through minor encroachments of the sea over a considerable period rather than by one sudden cataclysm, and it may be that the legend of lost Lyonnesse represents in distorted form the folk-memory of one such inundation. The forest of Mount's Bay is believed to have been flooded in the 11th century; it is not unreasonable to suppose that the valley between Tresco and St. Mary's was also flooded about this time.

The earliest record of human habitation in Scilly comes from the Bronze Age, and on nearly all the islands there can be found sepulchral barrows, passage graves and cists (stone boxes), in which the remains of Bronze Age dead were laid. The very large number of such chambered tombs (at one count about forty-seven entrance graves and over 200 barrows) has led to the suggestion that Scilly might be identified with the Isles of the Blest, where dead heroes of the ancient world were carried to rest in peace; but more likely explanations for their unusual number are that the practice of collective inhumation persisted in Scilly long after other regions had adopted cremation and single interment, and that fewer burial sites have been cleared by farmers than on the mainland. Attempts have also been made to identify Scilly with the Cassiterides, the secret islands where the Phoenicians obtained their tin, but this is no longer accepted.

Among the more recent archaeological finds have been huts of the Bronze Age and Early Iron Age at Knackyboy Carn and also some below the sand on Par Beach, Higher Town Bay, St. Martin's; the ancient village at Bant's Carn consisting of eleven huts dating from about the 2nd century B.C.; and a cemetery of ten oval cists containing grave goods, unearthed when the foundations of the council houses at Porthcressa were being dug in 1949. In 1962, gales did much damage in Scilly, and in 1995/96 the sea wall at Porthcressa was strengthened, as were the defences at Popplestones, Bryher, where the sea was threatening to cut the island in two. In 1962 gales swept away part of the sandbank on Nornour, revealing the foundations of several round

Bishop Rock Lighthouse Photo: David Rogers.

BISHOP ROCK LIGHTHOUSE

The Bishop Rock Lighthouse is the first bit of land usually sighted by passengers on ships after crossing the Atlantic and heading up the English Channel. Laurence Binyon wrote that it was:

Beautiful, dark and solitary,
The first of England that spoke to me.

It is perched on Scilly's westernmost rock, and has served as the finishing-post of the Blue Riband of the Atlantic races between the great liners. Until 1992 there were three keepers on it (each spent two months there, then one month ashore on the Garrison), and the summer launch trips to it used to take mail and newspapers to them. Now, a helicopter pad on its top caters for periodic servicing visits (see page 60).

The Bishop is made of Cornish granite, deemed harder than Scilly's, although one course, about halfway up, is of Irish granite. William Douglas was the engineer who accomplished the Bishop's construction with no lives lost; while in Scilly, he married one of the Miss Tregarthens. The Wolf rivals the Bishop in exposure to heavy seas, while landbased lights, such as Round Island, were considered by keepers a relatively soft posting:

Flashed Wolf to Round Island
'Oh you upon dry land,
With wild rabbits cropping the pinks
at your base,
You lubber you oughter
Stand watch in salt water,
With tides tearing at you and spray
in your face.'

– Crosbie Garstin.

huts. A quantity of Roman coins, bronze and enamel brooches, pieces of pottery, and glass and clay figures was unearthed there, and these are now on exhibition in the Isles of Scilly Museum. Sea defences were strengthened on Nornour in 1989 in an attempt to delay further erosion.

English Heritage maintains nine sites on Scilly, including prehistoric burial chambers on St. Mary's at Porth Hellick Down, Innisidgen (two), and Bant's Carn (see map). Four forts are also preserved: on St. Mary's is Harry's Walls (started in 1551 before Star Castle, but never completed); while, on Tresco, there are the Old Blockhouse (1554), King Charles's Castle (1550–54), and Cromwell's Castle (1651).

Artists such as Turner have found in Scilly the scenes, and especially the colours, they sought, and writers such as Sir Walter Besant (who wrote *Armorel of Lyonesse*) and Sir Arthur Quiller-Couch (who wrote *Major Vigoureux*) have led the way to a host of novels concerning the islands. Milton, Spencer, Dryden, Scott, Swinburne, William Morris, and other poets have all found inspiration from the stories of the islands, while Tennyson has helped to preserve the legend of the lost land of Lyonesse, which, in fiction, submerged between Land's End and Scilly, drowning some men from Mordred's army who had slain King Arthur. In fact, the sea has separated Scilly from Land's End since the last ice age, ten thousand years ago, although much reduction of land area within and around the Scillies has occurred since then.

PLEASURE BOATING

Pleasure boating forms a major part of most visitors' holidays in Scilly. The activity started seriously in the 1920s with Albert Poynter's two boats *White Hope* and *White Heather* and then the *Zedora*, later rivalled by Vernon Thompson's boats *Visitor* and *Springfield*. But each of these was licensed to carry only twelve passengers, a legal restriction sometimes circumvented by towing one or more barges loaded with passengers. Later, many larger boats were bought, and, in 1958, a co-operative association of most of the boatmen on St. Mary's was formed giving even better service than in the previous days of competition.

Scilly boatmen are particularly characterised by their skill at handling their boats, by their humour and ready wit, and by their great fund of knowledge, for they perform as unpaid guides with selfless and cheerful competence.

By 2004 the principal launches in the Boatmen's Association were skippered as follows:

Sea Horse – Stephen Hicks
Britannia – David Badcock
Osprey – Andy Howells
Golden Spray – Roy Duncan
Guiding Star – Joseph Badcock
Kingfisher of St. Mary's – Alec Hicks
Saphire – Joe Pender
Meridian – Jeremy Phillips
Sea King – Fraser Hicks
Surprise – Gerald Thompson

All the above launches have ship-to-shore radio telephone and carry safety equipment. Most also have a public address system and a toilet.

Until recently, Scillonian pleasure-launches included two which had a proud wartime history, in that they rescued hundreds of troops from the beaches of Dunkirk in 1940. These were the *Commodore* of Bryher, now restored and operating for the disabled out of Margate, and the *Southern Queen*, predecessor of the *Kingfisher of St. Mary's*, towed to Penzance in 1997 for restoration at Rospeath.

The **Nag's Head** is a prominent, lichen-covered granite rock on the downs of St. Agnes, weathered over ages to its present equine resemblance – at least in its forepart. The 18th century antiquarian, Dr. William Borlase, was fond of seeing the formation of these peculiarly-shaped rocks in Scilly as the work of druids, but, nowadays, we regard the shapes as the result of the actions of wind, rain and other natural phenomena over time, rather than involving human fashioning.

The Nag's Head (left) and (below) The Archdruid's Chair.
Photos: Keith Dibley

Challenging directions for finding the **Archdruid's Chair** were given in the 1920s by Herbert and Alexander Gibson, and on which the following is based. From **Porth Hellick Burial Mound** – which is easily found – proceed back on the path towards Porth Hellick for about 30 paces until an inconspicuous path among the heather appears on the left; follow this path roughly eastwards for about 120 paces to a large isolated boulder; turn right here over the heather for about 22 paces to a stone-basin lying in the ground and known as the **Sacred Bowl**; turn about 45 degrees leftwards here and strike off over the heather for about 120 paces to a larger rock alongside the coastal path but on its seaward side and known as the **Sun Rock**. Turn eastwards here towards the sea, and over the intervening heather, the back of the **Archdruid's Chair** should be clearly visible around 15 paces away. It is a perfect seat with arms and footstool – a most suitable spot from which to watch sunrise at the Summer Solstice. A less-challenging way of finding the **Archdruid's Chair** is to follow the coastal path until reaching the Sun Rock – but this loses some of the fun on the way.

To the north of the **Archdruid's Chair** and more difficult to spot is the former **Loaded Camel**, which has lost a distinguishing part of itself; the new **Loaded Camel** is at Porth Hellick. Some visitors seeking the **Archdruid's Chair** may have no compass with them. However, if it is a reasonably sunny day it may help to know that the direction of north can be found by laying one's analogue watch upon the ground with the hour-hand pointing in the general direction of the sun; then, by mentally bisecting the angle between the hour-hand and the straight line drawn from the watch-centre through 12 o'clock, the resulting bisector will run north-south. (If British Summer Time is in operation, the hour-hand should be set back one hour to Greenwich Mean Time, but that adjustment can be made mentally without altering the hands).

The *Southern Queen* is also known for enabling William Joyce to escape to Germany by secretly ferrying him across the English Channel from Folkestone just before the Second World War, so evading police checks at Dover. Joyce broadcast enemy propaganda to Britain during the war, being known as 'Lord Haw-Haw'; but his distinctive nasal tones gave him away in Denmark after the war, and he was brought back to Britain, tried and executed. Coincidently, Joyce had been brought up in the same place – Oldham – as Albert Pierrepoint, his executioner.

The launch *Firethorn* was built in 1991 and has a bow-operating door, enabling passengers to disembark straight on to a beach if desired, so removing any need to ferry people ashore in a punt or via a gangplank when landing on the uninhabited islands. This used to be required at low water even on Bryher because Church Quay dries out; but, in 1990, a new jetty running down the landing beach at Bar was built in a few days in the BBC television programme *Challenge Anneka* starring Anneka Rice, and has acquired the nickname *Annequay*. The *Firethorn* is built of steel with twin 180 h.p. diesel engines giving a top speed of twelve knots. She can carry up to 100 passengers, thirty of whom can be accommodated under cover – a boon to Bryher primary school children who make the crossing every schoolday in all weathers to attend Tresco School. The fastest Bryher boat is the jet *Cyclone* (30 knots) rivalled by the *Spearfish* of St. Mary's, which can reach St. Agnes in five minutes.

Passengers up to a total of twelve may also be carried in the Isles of Scilly Steamship Company's 52-foot, steel-built launch *Lyonesse Lady*, which supplies the off-islands with freight and mail throughout the year. She is the only vessel in Scilly launched by Her Majesty the Queen.

A number of new launches began operating in Scilly in the 1990s. Replacing the 1926 *Southern Queen* was the 1995 Falmouth-built *Kingfisher of St. Mary's*, fifty feet long with two Perkins engines and able to carry up to eighty passengers. St. Agnes Boating had the *Spirit of St. Agnes*, the first of the Nelson class of catamarans built at Cowes, with a speed of ten knots and able to carry eighty passengers, twenty-eight under shelter. At the same time the *Voyager of St. Martin's* came into service, a 56½-foot long mono-hull which cruises at about ten knots and carries up to 100 passengers, twenty-five of whom are seated under shelter. The new Hicks' launch *Sea Horse* entered service in 1997. She is of all-wood construction, fifty-eight feet long, built at Porthloo, and can carry up to 100 passengers, her larch planking coming from the Queen's estate at Balmoral. In 2001 came the *Sapphire*, replacing the *Lily of Laguna*, and in 2003 *Meridian* replaced *Kingsley II* and *Osprey* replaced *Buccaneer*, the two last old launches leaving to serve at Falmouth, delivering passengers to the National Maritime Museum from Penryn.

FISHING

Fishing around Scilly has increased, especially for Crab, Lobster, and Crawfish (the French **Langouste**). Catches of the local boats are of Megrim, Plaice, Ray, Monkfish and John Dory. Also caught are Mackerel, Conger, Coley, Scallop, Squid, Sole, Skate, Turbot, Hake, Cod, Brill, Mullet, Dogfish, Sprat and Ling (Nelson's favourite). Wrasse can be caught off the rocks, and there is a shoal called Powhl lying about six miles south-west of St. Agnes, a bank on the seabed which is what is left of an island submerged long ago and now a good area for Tunny, Pollock and others at slack tides in easy weather.

Sea Urchins (Sea Hedgehogs) are usually collected by skin divers at depths of several fathoms. They live on seaweed and shellfish, and their creamy roes are edible. Sea Urchin skeletons are popular for making into table lamps and ornaments.

OTHER BOOKS ON SCILLY

published by:
BOWLEY PUBLICATIONS LTD
P.O. Box 1, St. Mary's, Isles of Scilly, TR21 0PR

The FORTUNATE ISLANDS: the Story of the Isles of Scilly, 9th edition, containing chapters on the lost land of Lyonesse, the Vikings in Scilly, Wrecks and Lighthouses, Kelping, the Flower Industry, Robert Maybee, Legends, Folklore, Customs etc., and including photographs, Appendix, Bibliography and Index.

£7·50

SCILLY AT WAR, The Scillies consist of a cluster of 56 small islands – and many more rocks – in an area of Atlantic Ocean about 7 miles by 5, and situated about 25 miles WSW of Land's End. Only five islands are inhabited, by a relatively prosperous population of around 2,000, and the islands represent today a pleasant and different UK holiday location for visitors seeking to get away from crowds, crime, cars (including their own) and mainland concerns. In Scilly life seems a little closer to nature, but without sacrifice on the inhabited islands of the comforts of good hotels, pubs, guest houses, restaurants and cafés.

In the past the situation was different. The middle of the 17th century saw the English Civil Wars, and the first part of the book tells the story of Robert Blake and his conquest of Scilly in 1651, illustrated by some contemporary letters and first-hand accounts. The second part is concerned with the First World War, and includes the part played by seaplanes at their base on Tresco in helping to counter the U-boat menace. Developments in air travel between the wars concludes the second part. The third part is concerned with the Second World War and how it affected Scilly, and with the post-war travel developments to Scilly by sea and air.

'A fascinating, maverick but completely engaging smorgasbord of a book' – Cornish World, issue 27

ISBN 0-900184-34-5 – **£9·60**

The above two books are available from all good booksellers, or post free direct from the publisher above if ordering a single copy without discount from an address in the UK.

The whole Atlantic
Amassed recoils
And in indolent thunder
Bursts and boils. – L. Binyon

Photo: Keith Dibley

One of the attractions of the Scillies is how different they can feel to almost everywhere else in England. They consist mostly of tiny projections of granite out of the sea, unfashioned by man, the few larger ones with thin soil fringed by rocky shores and some unspoilt sandy beaches. On sunny summer days, they have clean air, clear visibility, bright light, vivid colourings, and an exhilarating freshness borne by salt-laden breezes – some of this conveyed in the photograph above.

Writers about the Scillies from the past have adored the Islands quite as much as many visitors do today. The Reverend H. J. Whitfield, writing in 1852, commented that he 'came for . . . three weeks, and stayed for three months. The beauty of the Islands, and the kindness I received at all hands, made those three months the happiest I ever spent in my life'. J. G. Uren in 1907 wrote 'Scilly is an ideal place' and 'fulfils all the conditions of a first-class sanatorium'. J. Mothersole, writing in 1910, quoted an American visitor to the Islands who had remarked 'you haven't learnt to hustle here. If the Islands belonged to us, we'd soon make things spin' – an observation which provoked a Scillonian to retort 'and could you hustle the tide?'

Most fulsome was S. P. B. Mais writing in 1928 who, quoting the poet Swinburne, described the Islands as this 'small sweet world of wave-encompassed wonder'.

SCILLY SHREWS CARAVANNING (see page 53)

The Scilly Shrew (*Crocidura suaveolens cassiteridum*) is occasionally seen in Scilly at the top of beaches foraging for insects such as sandhoppers. It lives for only about a year, and is found nowhere else in the UK. Remarkably, the Greater White-toothed Shrew is the only shrew on Guernsey, Alderney and Herm, while the Lesser White toothed Shrew is the only shrew on Jersey, Sark and Scilly, while Ireland has only one Shrew, the Pygmy Shrew.

CLIMATE DATA for the Isles of Scilly (1990s)

	January	February	March	April	May	June	July	August	September	October	November	December	Average for year
Average mid-month offshore sea temperatures (Celsius)	10	9	9	10	11	13	15	16	15	14	12	11	–
Average monthly maximum temperatures (Celsius)	9	9	11	12	14	17	19	19	17	15	12	10	14
Average monthly minimum temperatures (Celsius)	6	6	7	7	9	12	13	14	13	11	9	7	9
Average monthly rainfall (mm)	91	71	69	46	56	49	61	64	67	80	96	94	844
Average monthly sunshine hours	62	81	130	192	235	228	207	208	155	121	76	57	1752
Average monthly sunshine hours at Kew, London. Included for comparison	46	64	113	160	199	213	198	188	142	98	53	40	1514

SHRIMPING AND PRAWNING

Shrimping and prawning can be carried out at low tide, but, to help preserve stocks, the Marine Park Management Committee (consisting of representatives from the Isles of Scilly Environmental Trust, the Duchy of Cornwall, the Isles of Scilly Sea Fisheries Committee and English Nature), has resolved that shrimping and prawning be limited to the months of July, August and September.

VISITING YACHTS, WATER PURSUITS and the HARBOURS

Visiting yachts are catered for by thirty-eight swinging moorings in St. Mary's Harbour situated east of an imaginary straight line drawn between the lifeboat anchorage and the lifeboat slip. Vessels may not anchor immediately west of the anchored lifeboat – as this is *Scillonian III's* turning area – or near the end of the lifeboat slip. Alternative anchorages are in Porthcressa Bay, Tresco Channel, Teän Sound, St. Helen's Pool, and at the Cove or Perconger on St. Agnes. In St. Mary's Harbour the top permitted speed is three knots, and windsurfing and waterskiing in the harbour are not allowed. Jet-skiing and the use of spear-guns are not permitted anywhere in Scilly's Marine Park. On St. Mary's quay, on the noticeboard outside the harbourmaster's office, the times of high and low water are posted, together with the heights of the tides and a forecast of local weather for the day. The Pilotage Act of 1987 requires all vessels (except private craft under thirty metres in length, small trawlers and H.M. ships) to have a pilot on board or in close attendance when within six nautical miles of the southernmost tip of Samson.

SOME EPISODES FROM SCILLY'S HISTORY

A.D. 927. There is a legend that the Anglo-Saxon King Athelstan, after completing the English conquest of Cornwall at a battle near St. Buryan in about 927, then sailed to Scilly, defeating the Vikings there and founding a monastic cell on Tresco. But there is no evidence that Athelstan ever visited Scilly.

989. There is a legend that Olaf Tryggvesson, King of Norway, came to the Scillies after his Viking raiding around the British coast, and was converted to Christianity. Upon returning to Norway, he obliged his subjects also to adopt Christianity – at the point of his sword. But there is no evidence for this fine story, which was probably a subsequent invention, and appears in the *Heimskringla* of 1222, a saga by the Icelander, Snorri Sturlason. Olaf Tryggvesson was a figure of many such legends; in the year 1000 during a sea battle, he is said to have leapt overboard and was never seen again.

1114. Henry I granted Tresco and neighbouring islands to the Abbey of Tavistock, including a Benedictine priory to St. Nicholas which had been established on Tresco.

1306. Scilly leased at a yearly rent consisting partly of 6*s*. 8*d*. or 300 puffins.

1337. The Isles of Scilly were included in the Duchy of Cornwall and given, as part of the Honor of Launceston, to the Black Prince, who had been made Duke of Cornwall by his father Edward III.

1345. Welsh troops, aboard ships on their way to the Continent to fight for Edward III in the Hundred Years War 1337–1453, were becalmed close to Scilly. In starving conditions they landed and robbed the islanders at will.

1367. The Prior of Tresco reported that he could no longer repair all the priory buildings damaged and looted by pirates.

1570. Queen Elizabeth leased the islands to Francis Godolphin.

1646. Prince Charles, afterwards Charles II, took refuge for six weeks at Star Castle after the first Civil War before escaping to Jersey.

1648–51. In these years Scilly was in rebellion and the islands became a nest of privateers in the hands of rebellious Royalists under Sir John Grenville, passing ships being plundered regardless of their nationality.

1651. In this year the Dutch were so incensed by the piracies upon their ships committed by the Royalist rebels in Scilly that they sent a fleet of a dozen Men-of-War under Admiral Maarten Tromp (his name never included 'van') with the object not of declaring war upon Scilly but of seeking restitution. He arrived at Scilly shortly before an English fleet under Admiral Robert Blake, who was under Government orders to subdue the rebels. Tromp offered to help but Blake refused this, and proceeded, without either great preponderance of force or excessive 'effusion of blood', to suppress 'the dangerous nest of pirates', thus freeing the inhabitants of Scilly from the burden of trying to support so many diehard Royalists and their mainly Irish soldiery. What the islanders suffered under the rebel occupation cannot be measured but may be imagined; but, by masterly tactics and the offer of magnanimous terms, Blake successfully induced Sir John Grenville's surrender and ended a period of extreme privation under the Royalist occupation.

1742–1834. There was very poor living for most of the inhabitants in this period, and they relied mostly on fishing, kelping and smuggling.

1743. John Wesley visited Scilly from St. Ives and preached in Hugh Town.

Juliet's Garden.

Among the pleasures of a summer holiday in Scilly are the many places and opportunities for eating outdoors – fresh crab salads and cream teas are favourites – often in gardens remote from all traffic. Each of the four inhabited off-islands has such places including Coastguard's Café, Covean Cottage and the Turk's Head on St. Agnes, Fraggle Rock Restaurant, Vine Cottage and Hell Bay Hotel on Bryher, Seven Stones Inn, Polreath Tea Rooms, and the Hotel on St. Martin's, the garden of the New Inn, the Island Hotel terrace, the Quay Shop Café and the Abbey Gardens Café on Tresco. On St. Mary's outside Hugh Town are Old Town Café, Tolman Café, the Heritage Centre at Longstone and Juliet's Garden Café above Porthloo, seen in the photograph above. Tea may also be taken on the terrace of the Porthcressa Inn and Restaurant, in the garden of the Corner House Restaurant (Scilly Plaice), in the small garden of Tregarthen's Hotel, where Alfred, Lord Tennyson is credited with composing part of his poem *Enoch Arden*, or on the 16th century ramparts of Star Castle Hotel, or at Carn Vean naer Pelistry, at the buffet at St. Mary's Airport, at the *dibble and grub* at the eastern end of Porthcressa – or, in high summer, a fish-and-chip van is parked behind the Town Hall, providing 'a sup on the sands', if desired.

1810. Trinity House took over pilotage in Scilly. (In 1810 there were seventy-six licensed pilots; in 2004 there were two.)
1831. The Duke of Leeds (Godolphin) did not renew the lease, so Scilly reverted to the Duchy of Cornwall.
1834. Augustus Smith obtained the lease of the islands from the Duchy and became Lord Proprietor. The prosperity of the islands dates from the arrival of this energetic and far-seeing Hertfordshire squire. Augustus Smith built the house called Tresco Abbey near the site of the old priory on Tresco, and laid out the Abbey Gardens.
1790–1880. Shipbuilding was an industry in Scilly. There were five shipbuilding yards on St. Mary's between 1835 and 1871 and the industry prospered until iron vessels replaced wooden ones, and steam had replaced sail.
1858. Penzance to Scilly steam ferry began. Bishop Rock lighthouse began functioning.
1859. Great Western Railway extended to Penzance; excursion trips to Scilly followed.
1900–04. *HMS Dreadnought* was arguably the most important ship in Scilly's history, but not for any usual reasons. She never visited the Islands, and it was not her speed of construction in 1906 which was relevant – even if no other capital ship was ever built in so short a time; nor was it much to do with her ten all-big guns, for she never fired these at an enemy in her whole career; but it was partly connected with the weight of these 12-inch guns and with her thick armour, for it was Dreadnought's draught which was the crucial factor – she was just too deep in the water for safe navigation of St. Mary's Sound at low tides. *Dreadnought* made all existing battleships obsolescent, and meant that subsequent battleships would also draw more water. This led to the Admiralty's decision to abandon its plans to make Scilly a great naval base, and the projected breakwater and naval dockyard were cancelled. Up to £¼ million had already been spent in Scilly, 1900-04, on protective forts, such as the one at Steval on the Garrison, which was equipped with two 12-pounder guns; but no more money was allocated, and Scapa Flow was developed instead – a lucky escape for Scilly.
1914–18. Seaplanes and flying-boats of 34 Squadron, Royal Navy Air Service were based first at Porthmellon in 1917 and then at New Grimsby to counter the U-boats.
1918. Major A. A. Dorrien Smith, D.S.O., succeeded his father and, in 1920, his lease of all islands except Tresco was relinquished to the Duchy.
1930s. Two capital ships of the Royal Navy paid extended visits to Scilly in the pre-war years. One was the graceful, 42,000 ton battlecruiser 'the mighty *Hood*', the greatest warship in the world between the wars and the epitome of Britain's seapower. On 24th May 1941, *Hood* engaged the cruiser *Prinz Eugen* in the mistaken belief that she was the German battleship *Bismarck*; but *Prinz Eugen* scored the first hits, starting a fire on *Hood*. Then *Bismarck*, which was following *Prinz Eugen* found *Hood's* range, and with her third salvo caused *Hood* to blow up, with the loss of 1,418 crew – only three surviving, each found clinging to a separate Carley float. The other capital ship visiting Scilly was the 33,000 ton battleship *Rodney*, 6th–10th July, 1930, which in 1941 avenged the *Hood's* loss by playing a major part with her nine 16-inch guns in silencing the guns of the *Bismarck*, even firing torpedoes at the *Bismarck*, the only occasion in history when a battleship has attempted to torpedo another battleship. Eventually, on 27th May, *Bismarck's* German crew scuttled their ship to prevent her capture, but only 113 men survived out of her complement of about 2,300.
1937. First scheduled air service of twin-engined De Havilland Dragon biplanes to St. Mary's from St. Just began on 15th September using two fairways on the golf course as

landing strips. The present airport opened in 1939.

1939. From 27th June to 3rd July, 1933, the 22,500 ton aircraft carrier *Courageous* was in Scilly during which, with concerts, dances, tours of the ship, a variety show given by the ship's company in the Town Hall, and in many sporting events, the warship's crew endeared themselves to the Islanders. The sinking of *Courageous*, torpedoed by U29 on 17th September, 1939, while she was on anti-submarine patrol some 200 miles west of the Bishop Rock, was especially sad in Scilly as 518 of the 1,200 crew were lost. The U-boat commander, Otto Schuhart, evaded the heavy depthcharging of *Courageous'* four escorting destroyers and, when U-29 returned to Wilhelmshaven, was welcomed at the quayside by Hitler.

1941. Hurricane fighter aircraft of 87 Squadron RAF were based on St. Mary's.

1941–45. The Scillies became a base for air/sea rescue craft during the Second World War in the Battle of the Atlantic against German submarines. U681 struck the Crim Rocks on 11th March, 1945, and was holed. The U-boat's whereabouts on the ocean floor was discovered by divers in 1999, and some items brought to the surface. Another submarine, U1209, was similarly holed after diving too close to the Wolf Rock on 18th December, 1944.

1949. The Duchy of Cornwall offered the freehold of its properties in Hugh Town to sitting tenants. Most tenants subsequently took up the offer.

1952. The fastest, regular commercial crossing of the Atlantic was made by the 51,988 ton liner *United States* at an average speed of 35·39 knots, so winning the Hales Trophy for the Blue Riband of the Atlantic.

1954. Income tax introduced to Scilly for the first time.

1964. Two Sikorsky S61 helicopters flying from Penzance superseded De Havilland Dragon Rapides, seven-seater biplanes which had flown from Land's End.

1971. Motor taxation introduced in Scilly for the first time.

1974. Earliest wreck (1555) found in Scilly on Bartholomew Ledges.

1983. Tresco heliport opened.

1985. The inhabited off-islands received mains electricity – linked to St. Mary's by undersea cable.

1987. Skybus service began – Land's End Aerodrome to St. Mary's. The Duchy of Cornwall leased the uninhabited islands and untenanted land to the Isles of Scilly Wildlife Trust for a peppercorn rent.

1989. Mainland electricity came to Scilly by means of a thirty-six mile undersea cable.

1991. Airport runway extended, improving air safety.

1992. Water desalination plant built on St. Mary's, alleviating the water shortage.

1992. *Destriero* arrived after crossing the Atlantic in under 3 days.

1998. A bottle was retrieved from the sea at Hell Bay on Bryher, which had been released into the sea at Newfoundland (nearly 2,000 miles away) 387 days previously. The bottle contained a message from a 10-year-old girl seeking a penfriend; another bottle landing on Bryher in 1962 had a sadder message; it was from a lone French yachtsman in mid-Atlantic asking for 'something strong to drink and someone to make love to'.

1998. Alison Streeter swam the twenty-six miles from Deep Point, St. Mary's, to Sennen beach, near Land's End, setting off at 4 a.m. and arriving at 7.30 p.m. escorted all the way by the launch *Sea Horse*, from which she was supplied with hot drinks en route.

*Walking the clean sands, paddling in the clear sea, or just messing about in a boat – timeless, tireless pastimes in Pentle Bay, Tresco. 'It's the **only** thing,' said the Water Rat solemnly...'Believe me...there is **nothing** – absolutely nothing – half so much worth doing as simply messing about in boats.' – Chap 1,* Wind in the Willows, *Kenneth Grahame.*

Photo: C. Rogers

Alison had already swum the English Channel thirty-seven times.

1999–2001. New gigs *Tregarthen, Galatea* and *Dauntless* were built in Scilly. Brewing of the 'Ales of Scilly' began.

2001. A lifesize, wooden figure of a neo-classical warrior was found on the seabed off Samson from the stern of *Colossus*. It has survived 249 years underwater. Later in the year, baby Jacob was safely delivered in a BI helicopter *en route* to Penzance.

2003. A duty traffic warden visited Hugh Town for a day in October and cautioned a number of drivers to belt up. One parking ticket was issued. A new medical launch *Star of Life* was acquired for Scilly.

2004. Freehold property prices in Scilly rose to over twice those of similar properties in mainland Cornwall. One problem in Scilly is that essential public-service workers experience difficulty in obtaining affordable housing in the Islands, where the proportion of properties available for letting to holidaymakers is one of the highest in the UK. There has also been a diminution of council houses – only about 108 by 2003 – a problem not peculiar to Scilly, for the statutory right of tenants to buy their council houses was a politically popular measure introduced nationally by the Thatcher administration. Since about 1990 approximately 50,000 Council houses in the UK have been sold annually to sitting tenants, with only about 30,000 new ones built annually, so worsening the situation.

Present Day: The inhabitants today welcome visitors whether they come to see the flowers, to watch the magnificent spectacle of an Atlantic storm, to study the birds, to sail the inland sea, to bathe in the sandy bays, or come, as so many do, to find a measure of tranquillity in the sun.

They stretched in never-ending line
Along the margin of a bay:
Ten thousand saw I at a glance,
Tossing their heads in sprightly dance.
Wordsworth

For over a hundred years flower farming has been one of the main occupations in Scilly.
Photo: Gibson, Scilly

THE ISLANDS OF SCILLY

The following is a list of the fifty-six islands of the Isles of Scilly. The definition of an island – for the purposes of this list – is land surrounded by water at high tide, supporting a variety of land vegetation at all times, and locally accepted as an island.

Annet
Bryher
Burnt Island
Castle Bryher
Crow Island
Crump Island
Foreman's Island
Great Arthur
Great Ganilly
Great Ganinick
Great Innisvouls
Green Island (off Samson)
Green Island (off Tresco)
The Gugh
Guther's Island
Gweal
Hedge Rock
Hangman Island
Illiswilgig
Innisidgen
Little and Middle Arthur
Little Ganilly
Little Ganinick
Little Innisvouls
Men-a-vaur
Menawethan
Merrick Island (New Grimsby)
Merrick Island (Stony Porth)
Mincarlo
Newford Island
Nornour
Northwethel
Old Man
Outer Colvel Rock
Peashopper Island
Pednbrose
Pernagie
Plumb Island (off St. Martin's)
Plumb Island (off Tresco)
Puffin Island
Rosevean
Rosevear
Round Island
St. Agnes (or Agnes)
St. Helen's
St. Martin's
St. Mary's
Samson
Shipman Head
Taylor's Island
Teän
Tins Walbert
Toll's Island (Cat Island in 1600)
Tresco
White Island (off St. Martin's and pronounced 'wit')
White Island (off Samson and pronounced 'wight')

The distinctive eighty-five feet high rock *Hanjague* (pronounced 'Han'jig' and spoken of as 'the Sugar Loaf') is east of Scilly and surrounded by relatively deep water. Lack of sufficient vegetation disqualifies it for inclusion in the list of islands, but it could once have been a high point of the legendary lost land of Lyonnesse, said to have been inundated by the sea hereabouts – unless this was at Leonois off Brittany.

TOURS, ACTIVITIES AND TAXIS

There are a number of operators offering coach or minibus tours around St. Mary's lasting about 1¼ hours. They usually start from Porthcressa Bank and include:

	Telephone
Classic Car Tours	01720 422479
Open Top Tours by doubledecker	01720 422901
Heritage Tours	01720 422387
Windsurfing and Sailing	01720 422037

TAXIS are as follows:

Island Taxis	01720 422635 or 422126
Lukes Taxi	01720 423424
Minstral Cabs	01720 422460 or 07787 115343
Q-Cabs	01720422260
Scilly Cabs	01720 422901
St. Mary's Taxis	01720 422555

Scilly's own magazine is **The Scillonian**, published half-yearly and available from the newsagent, C. Mumford, Hugh Street, St. Mary's. Read it to keep in touch.

SKIMMING

Skimming a flattish pebble from the beach out on the surface of a calm sea, so that it bounces on the water before finally sinking, is a harmless pastime but demands a skilful flick of the wrist. The record for the number of bounces achieved is 38, won in 2002 on a ripple-free river surface. An unexpected help is to select stones which are not completely smooth, but have some small pits in them to reduce drag – rather in the way that indentations on a golfball serve to lessen air drag – smoothness in such sports not being everything.

KING ARTHUR??

King Arthur, the heroic British defender against the English, is a figure of powerful legend rather than proven history, a leader from the dark ages of British history where much in the record is uncertain. After his defeat and mortal wounding at the *Battle of Camlann* in about the year 537 A.D., Arthur is said to have been taken by barge to his final resting-place on Avalon. If this is identified as part of the Scillies, then his burial may have been on the westward-facing slopes of Great Arthur. The following are relevant extracts from Alfred, Lord Tennyson's poem *Morte D'Arthur*:

So all day long the noise of battle rolled
Among the mountains by the winter sea;
Until King Arthur's table, man by man,
Had fall'n in Lyonnesse about their Lord,

But now farewell. I am going a long way
With these thou seëst–if indeed I go–
(For all my mind is clouded with a doubt)
To the island-valley of Avilion;
Where falls not hail, or rain, or any snow,
Nor ever wind blows loudly; but it lies
Deep-meadowed, happy, fair with orchard-lawns
And bowery hollows crowned with summer sea,
Where I will heal me of my grievous wound.'
So said he, and the barge with oar and sail
Moved from the brink, like some full-breasted swan
That, fluting a wild carol ere her death,
Ruffles her pure cold plume, and takes the flood
With swarthy webs. Long stood sir Bedivere
Revolving many memories, till the hull
Looked one black dot against the verge of dawn,
And on the mere the wailing died away.

(Tennyson's penultimate line suggests that the barge sailed eastwards towards the dawning sun – rather than westwards to Scilly; moreover, '*nor ever wind blows loudly*' does not sound like Scilly where it certainly can. In the 6th century the present island of Great Arthur was likely to have been a hill on the island of Ennor, which, before the sea invaded its valleys, encompassed the majority of the present islands of Scilly).

Pollution can sometimes become a thing of beauty, as when, in still, summer skies, sunbeams pierce the dust, scattering red wavelengths to create particularly spectacular Scillonian sunsets. *Photo: Keith Dibley*

Common Prawn – *(Leander serratus)* is a dainty crustacean with a transparent body which may be found in rock pools or creeping stealthily towards the shore on a flowing tide. Like a lobster it has five pairs of limbs, three for walking and two for grasping food. A pair of black eyes on top of movable stalks in its head provide all-round vision and, if startled, its relatively massive tail fan will propel the creature backwards through the water in a single lightning dart.

Mermaid's Purses

Rays lay their eggs in these cases in shallow water. The cases can be distinguished from those of the Dogfish by their pointed horns at each corner instead of coiled tendrils.

Sea Anemone – The Sea Anemone was called 'the flower animal' by the Greeks and its common form is the *Beadlet* which, when seen on the rocks exposed to the air by the receding tide, appears as a small blob of dark red jelly. But, when the sea covers it, it opens up and extends its tentacles which sway with the movement of the sea until a passing small fish approaches too close; then the anemone reveals itself as a ferocious carnivore, all tentacles grasping its victim until it has been devoured. The anemone will react in a similar manner to the touch of one's finger, but there is no danger of losing a member, for the anemone's poison, with which it paralyses its victims, is scarcely perceptible to humans as more than a vague sting, if that.

Anemones reproduce by sex or without it – the latter by detaching parts of themselves, a few of which then grow into adult anemones of male, female or both genders.

TRELAWNEY

GUEST HOUSE

Church Street, St. Mary's, Isles of Scilly, TR21 0JT

E-mail: dtownend@netcomuk.co.uk
Website: www.trelawney-ios.co.uk

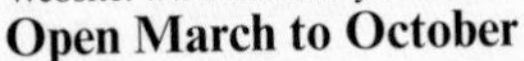

Open March to October

English Tourism Council ♦♦♦♦ GUEST ACCOMMODATION

A centrally-situated Guest House, established in 1969, with a friendly atmosphere and a menued breakfast · Rooms with private facilities · No smoking

Call in to see us for a brochure. Tel or Fax: David or Lyn on (01720) 422377

'SPORTS MODE'

The Parade (by the Park), St. Mary's
Tel: 01720 422293 Fax: 01720 422377
Website: www.sportsmode-ios.co.uk

– The Islands' only Sports Shop –

ISLES OF SCILLY

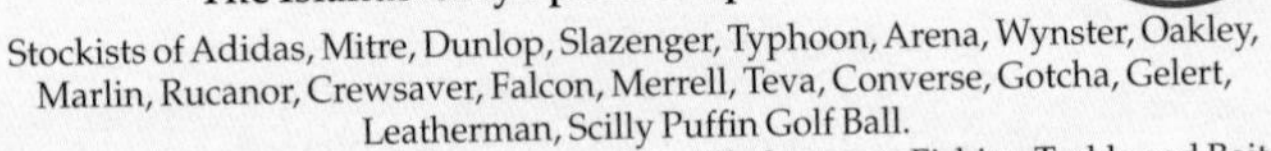

Stockists of Adidas, Mitre, Dunlop, Slazenger, Typhoon, Arena, Wynster, Oakley, Marlin, Rucanor, Crewsaver, Falcon, Merrell, Teva, Converse, Gotcha, Gelert, Leatherman, Scilly Puffin Golf Ball.

'For all your sporting needs' – pay us a visit · Shakespeare Fishing Tackle and Baits
Agents for Official World Gig Championship Shirts

BUCKINGHAM HOUSE

HUGH TOWN · ST. MARY'S

A comfortable guest-house situated one minute from the quay and shops.

Excellent Food, Table Licence, Comfortable Lounge, Hot & Cold Water, Shaving Points, Personal Attention. Open January to December.

S.A.E. for Brochure Mr. P. Malec

Telephone : Scillonia (01720) 422543

Find us through the Post Office arch

WATERLOO BOOKS

Well Lane, St. Mary's · Telephone: (01720) 422509

Old Prints and Postcards · Second-hand Books and Paperbacks

Items relating to Scilly

New stock always wanted – please ring for a quotation

THE WHEELHOUSE

Licensed Guest House

SITUATED RIGHT ON PORTHCRESSA BEACH
EIGHT BEDROOMS, ALL WITH PRIVATE FACILITIES
SIX BEDROOMS WITH SEA VIEWS · GOOD FOOD AND PERSONAL SERVICE IN COMFORTABLE SURROUNDINGS
OPEN ALL YEAR ROUND · TOTALLY NON SMOKING

Proprietress: Liz Heslin

Porthcressa, St. Mary's, Isles of Scilly. Telephone: 01720 422719

Lyonnesse Guest House

The Strand, St. Mary's
Isles of Scilly
TR21 0PS

Lyonnesse is a Grade II listed building, which has been carefully updated to provide spacious, attractive and comfortable accommodation. The front rooms, lounge and dining-room have superb views over the harbour and off-islands, and the beach is just yards from the front door.

At Breakfast, and for Dinner every evening, our aim is to provide the widest variety of traditional, imaginative meals using fresh local produce whenever possible, and carefully cooked on our Aga.

Awarded 3-diamonds by the ETC and recommended by our guests.

For a brochure, please write to or phone

Mrs. M. Woodcock – Tel: 01720 422458

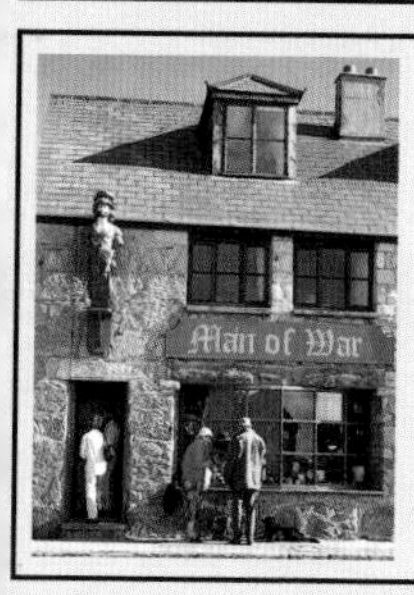

WARLEGGAN HOLIDAY FLATS

Modern and comfortable self-catering flats for two to six persons.
Fully equipped to a high standard.

For brochure please contact:

Mrs. C. Hiron, Warleggan, St. Mary's, Isles of Scilly

Telephone: **Scillonia (01720) 422563**

Man of War

ON THE STRAND, HUGH TOWN

An Aladdin's Cave of antiques and curiosities – and the chance to obtain GENUINE TREASURE COIN from local shipwrecks direct from the salvors.
Mail order available.

Telephone: **Scillonia (01720) 422563**

HARBOUR LIGHTS WITH SMUGGLER'S RIDE HOLIDAY FLATS

Thoroughfare, Hugh Town, St. Mary's, Isles of Scilly, TR21 0JN

Luxurious holiday apartments most with sea views situated by the beach. Self-catering flats available for holiday-lets all year round.

Details from: Mr. & Mrs. T. C. Clifford

Telephone and Facsimile: 01872 863537

Website: www.selfcateringislesofscilly.co.uk

EXCELLENT FOOD – SUPERB SERVICE

The hotel is informal, with a relaxed, friendly atmosphere. 23 EN SUITE BEDROOMS – all with direct dial telephone, TV, radio, tea/coffee maker, hairdryer. Single, twin, double and family rooms available. Also ground floor rooms and some with sea views. No smoking dining room and lounge.

QUIET CENTRAL POSITION *– 100 yards from Porthcressa and Town beaches, and a few minutes' walk from entertainments and the harbour.*

FULLY LICENSED *– Enjoy a quiet drink in the ISLAND ROOM LOUNGE BAR – open to non-residents. We look forward to seeing you. Do call in.*

EXCELLENT VALUE!

We have been looking after guests for nearly 100 years. Special low rate bargain breaks – early and late – call in and see us.

Open most of the year ~ Website: www.bellrockhotel.co.uk

MARINE HOUSE

Church Street, Hugh Town, St. Mary's, TR21 0JT

A small guesthouse offering Bed and Breakfast in comfortable accommodation.
Centrally situated close to beaches, shops and harbour. ETC registered 3 Diamonds.

THE CAPTAIN'S CABIN

Ram's Valley, St. Mary's

A first floor, very well appointed flat in a quiet part of town.
Linen, towels, colour television, etc. provided. Sleeps up to four people. ETC registered 3 Stars.

For further information contact: **Mike and Peggy Rowe**

Telephone: **01720 422966** **E-mail: peggy@rowe55.freeserve.co.uk**

Longstone Heritage Centre

St Marys – Open 10.00am to 5.00pm daily

Café – Homemade soup and cakes, hot and cold food served all day
Heritage Exhibition – Scilly past and present, a journey through time
Gift Shop – Quality gifts, books and local crafts
Wonderful views over Porth Hellick from our garden and terrace

Find us off Telegraph Road just up the lane from Carreg Dhu Gardens

Telephone : 01720 423770

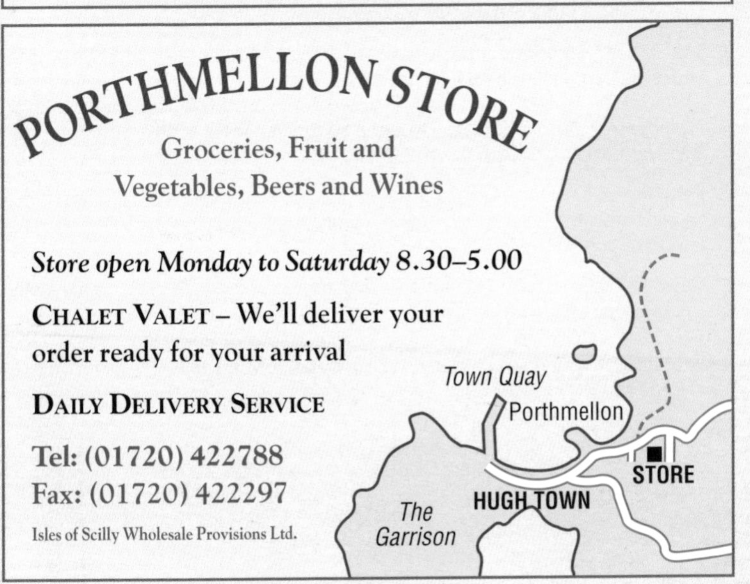

PORTHMELLON STORE
Groceries, Fruit and
Vegetables, Beers and Wines
Store open Monday to Saturday 8.30–5.00
CHALET VALET – We'll deliver your
order ready for your arrival
DAILY DELIVERY SERVICE
Tel: (01720) 422788
Fax: (01720) 422297
Isles of Scilly Wholesale Provisions Ltd.
Town Quay
Porthmellon
STORE
HUGH TOWN
The
Garrison

ACCOMMODATION IN ISLES OF SCILLY AND PENZANCE

1. **22 Sally Port**, St. Mary's, Isles of Scilly. A well-equipped house which sleeps six people and has excellent sea views. Write to: Island Properties, Porthmellon, St. Mary's, Isles of Scilly or telephone 01720 422082.

2. **Beachfield Hotel**, Promenade, Penzance, TR18 4NW, overlooks Mount's Bay with panoramic views. The hotel offers the highest-rated accommodation in Penzance, all rooms *en suite* with full facilities. Ideal for those 'Scilly bound'. Telephone: (01736) 362067. Fax: (01736) 331100. Website: www.beachfield.co.uk

2002/03

3. **Mrs. J. Lee**, Honeydew Guest House, 3 Leskinnick Street, Penzance, TR18 2HA. Situated directly opposite the Railway/Coach Station and close to the Heliport and *Scillonian III* ferry to the Isles of Scilly. Early breakfasts can be served by arrangement. Accommodation is all *en suite*, and there is also a family room. Bookings welcome. Telephone: 01736 364206.

4. **Glen Dower**, Bed and Breakfast, 5 Mennaye Road, Penzance, TR18 4NG. Telephone: Dave Evans on 01736 365991. Ideal accommodation at a reasonable price for visitors bound for the Scillies and on return.

5. When in Penzance, visit **The Buttery** restaurant in Alverton Street, recommended for 'the best roast lunch in town'.

Cover photo: *C. Rogers. The pleasure launch,* Kingfisher of St. Mary's, *leaving Higher Town Quay on St. Martin's, with Par Beach beyond – one of miles of beautiful, sandy beaches in the Scillies.*

Printed in England

Produced by Reef Publishing Ltd. Tel. 01736 333783

Published by:

Bowley Publications Ltd., P.O. Box 1, St. Mary's, Isles of Scilly, TR21 0PR.

Artist: Sue Dibley. *International Standard Book No. 0 900184 39 6.*